THE
CELTIC LEGEND
OF THE
BEYOND

THE CELTIC LEGEND OF THE BEYOND

BY
ANATOLE LE BRAZ

TRANSLATED BY
DEREK BRYCE

ISBN 9947992 06 5

English translation copyright ⊙. 1986.
Reprinted in 1991.
LLANERCH PUBLISHERS. FELINFACH.

Contents.

"As for the distinction which torments common man, that of life and death... Is not love of life an illusion? Is not fear of death an error? This departure, is it really a misfortune? Does it not lead, like the bride who leaves the paternal home, to another happiness?"

ZHUANG ZI*

*From Weiger, 'Wisdom of the Daoist Masters.'

Before the coming of Christianity, the Celtic peoples of Western Europe had strong and singular beliefs about the future life. In fact, it was their preoccupation with the beyond, which extended even to the making of loans to be settled in the 'other world,' which the Romans regarded as their most striking feature.

Caesar tells us that the Gauls claimed, on the authority of their Druids, to be descended from the God of Death, and it was for this reason that they measured the passage of time 'not by days, but by nights.' The same author tells us of the great importance they attached to funerals, which were sometimes exceptionally sumptuous, and that the main aim of the Druidic teaching to the people was the inculcation of the certitude that the soul survived. Pomponius Mela gives us to understand that the Druids kept most of their knowledge to themselves and their disciples, limiting themselves to preaching the idea of survival to the masses. In the 'Pharsalia,' Lucian, in a verse addressed to the Druids, wrote: 'According to your teaching, the shades do not go to the silent dwellings of Erebus, nor to the pale underground kingdoms of Pluto; the same spirit animates the limbs in another world; if your science is not charlatanism, death is the middle of a long life.'

In the fourth century A.D., Procopus wrote that on the coast opposite the Island of Britain there were many villages whose inhabitants grew crops, but were also fishermen. Subject to the Francs, they were free from payment of tribute because of a certain service which, they said, they had been performing since ancient times. This service, they claimed, was the transport of souls. At night, they would suddenly be awakened by a loud knocking at the door, and a voice outside would call them to their task. They would get up in haste and a mysterious force would drag them from their homes towards the beach, even against their will. There would be boats there, not their own, but others. They would look empty but, in reality, they would be loaded almost to the point of sinking and the water would be up to the gunnels. They would climb in and take the oars. An hour later, despite the invisible passengers' weight, they would reach the Island (of Britain) although the voyage would normally have taken a day and a half. Scarcely had they touched the coast than the boats would rise up without their seeing the passengers disembark, and the same voice that had called them would be heard. It was that of the conductor of souls

7

presenting the dead one by one to those qualified to receive
them, calling the men by their fathers' names, women, if
there were any, by their husbands' names, and describing
what they did when they were alive.

The above is a summary of the story given by Procopus;
it is the most complete account of the Celtic legend of
the dead that we have from the writings of Classical An-
tiquity.

There can be little doubt that many of the beliefs, practices and customs associated with the Celtic cult of the
dead passed into early Celtic Christianity. In Ireland, for
example, so many Christian monasteries appeared so quickly
after the conversion by Saint Patrick, as to imply the whole-
sale conversion of Druidic colleges.

In Britain, Archbishop Cranmer began the suppression of
the cult of the dead, saying the dead were either saved or
lost, and nothing more could be done once they were gone.
In the Celtic parts of the British Isles, many practices, and
beliefs survived until quite recent times, many of them
quite similar to ones given in this book; but in Brittany the
old traditions and practices survived longer and in a more
complete form; their suppression there being relatively recent.

Almost all the stories in this book are based on events
that actually took place, mostly in the nineteenth century.
Sometimes they are first hand accounts of personal psychic
experiences; sometimes they are further removed, and have
been embellished and dramatised, as in the story of the
drunken boy who stole a skull, and the tales of Tadic-coz, a
priest who really existed, but to whom the storytellers have
already given a superhuman and mythological character.

The content of many of these tales is often more psychic
than spiritual. Despite the recent origin of these tales, they
still have an archaic character, witnessed by their lack of
sentimental morality. The tales are told directly and fact-
ually, implying not so much the idea of reward and punish-
ment for good and bad deeds, as that some situations are
to be avoided simply because they are dangerous.

Derek Bryce,
Wales,
1986.

Chapter 1. Premonitions*.

There are premonitions which announce death, but the person who experiences them is rarely the one threatened by death.

If the premonition occurs in the morning, it means that the event announced will happen after a brief delay (eight days at the most); if in the evening, the due date is further off, even a year or more.

No one dies without a close relative, friend, or neighbour having been warned by a premonition.

Premonitions are like a shadow, projected beforehand, of what is going to happen.

If we were less preoccupied with what we are doing and with what is going on around us in this world, we would be in touch with almost everything that happened in the other.

Those who deny premonitions have just as many of them as the others. They deny them uniquely because they do not know how to see or hear them; perhaps also because they fear them and wish to see and hear nothing of the other life.

- § -

"Some people, more than others, have the gift of sight.

When I was young they pointed out to me, as though it were a dreadful secret, those who were gifted with this mysterious power.

'The one over there has the power,' they would say.

In this privileged category, one should put foremost those 'who have passed over consecrated ground and come out of it without having been christened.'

This is how it can happen:

A child comes to be born. The priest has arranged the time for the christening. But you know how bad the country folk are at time-keeping. The father, matron, and the god-parents lag on the way, stopping at any inns there may be, reaching the town long after the arranged time. The priest has become weary of waiting in vain or has been called away to some other task of his ministry. Our people reach the porch and find the church empty. In their turn they wait in vain. It is cold; the child is crying; the matron (crafty soul) says that if they stay there the newly-born will risk to 'catch its death of cold.' They go a more sheltered spot, the nearest inn. They wait there, emptying a pint, until the

*Omens, warning signs, appearances.

9

priest returns. The child has passed over the consecrated ground of the church cemetery and come out of it without having been made a Christian. He will have the gift of sight.

This often occurs and that is why so many Bretons have the faculty to see what is invisible to the majority of men."
(René Alain, Quimper.)

- § -

Eight premonitions of a single death.

"Each time one of my family has died, I have been warned by a premonition; but the premonitions which have struck me most, were those which preceded my husband's death. I had all kinds of them during the seven months his illness lasted.

One evening when I had watched over him till late, I had fallen asleep from tiredness on the seat next to the bed. I was suddenly awakened by a noise like that of a window opening. 'The wind must have blown it open,' I thought. A cool, humid breath passed over my face, as though it came from a cellar. I remembered that I had left some flax hanging outside to dry, and said to myself: 'I hope my flax hasn't blown away.'

I got up quickly. To my great surprise, the window was firmly shut. I went to the door and opened it. It was a clear starlit night. The flax was there, the trees held themselves motionless, and there was not a breath of wind.

I didn't worry much about this first event, even though it seemed mysterious to me. Several days later, at dusk, I was walking in the company of a neighbour, along the path from our door. Suddenly I heard my husband call from the other end of the house, where he was in bed close to the hearth. I ran.

'What's the matter?' I asked him.

He didn't reply, and I saw that he was in a deep sleep, his head turned towards the wall.

I went back to the neighbour.

'Did you hear Lucas call me just now?' - 'Yes.' - 'How do you explain that? He's sleeping there like a hibernating badger...'

A month or two went by. My man got neither better nor worse. One night, I had just stretched out alongside him and started to take some rest, when I heard the footsteps of someone walking stealthily in the attic, just above my head. Then it sounded as though several persons were whispering. Then there was a sound of planks being moved, followed by a repeated noise of a hammer driving nails.

It was all quite extraordinary, for the trap door to the attic had not been opened for a week, and, in any case, there was only a little oat chaff and some small faggots up there, and not a single plank.

I called out loud:

'Who's that making all this noise, preventing Christians from sleeping?'

Then I made the sign of the cross, and waited... But the noise had ceased as soon as I had spoken.

On the following day I went to the river to wash some sheets. There is no road, but a narrow path passing for most of its length between banks planted with trees. I was but a little way along the path when I heard footsteps and a sound of heavy breathing behind me, as well as a brushing of the overhanging branches. What was strange, was that I distinctly recognised my husband's steps, from the time when he was in good health, when he used to walk back home from one of the surrounding farms at the end of a day's work.

I turned round.

There was no one there!!!

I spent the morning washing. I heard nothing more on the way back, but the load of washing that I carried began to weigh so heavy on my shoulders that it could have been changed into lead. Since then, I have understood what it meant. Amongst the sheets was the one which would serve to shroud my poor, dear husband.

For Lucas died three days later. God had his soul! Those three days saw signs succeeding one another almost without interruption.

That night, the door was slamming violently, a hum of a crowd penetrated the house, and there was a sound of many footsteps going up and down the stairs. The following night, there was a sound of far-off bells ringing, a light burning with a pale flame at the head of the bed where we were lying, and then the singing of priests who were coming across the fields from the direction of the town.

I no longer dared close my eyes.

But it was the last night that was the most terrifying. My husband, who didn't seem any worse, had told me not to stay awake. When I was sure that he was resting, I tried to doze off myself. But right then I heard the jolting of a carriage. What made it more surprising was that there was no carriage road in the vicinity of our house. When we first moved in, we had to bring our furniture on a wheelbarrow. Yet the carriage was clearly coming towards our house. The squeaking of a badly-greased axle became more and more distinct. Soon I could hear it quite close by. I rose up on my knees. There was a little dormer window close to the bed. I looked through it, thinking to see the carriage go by. But I could see nothing except the moonlit air and the black shapes of the trees around the fields. The axle continued squeaking, and the carriage went on jolting. It went round the house a first time, then a second, and then for a third time. At the third circuit there was a heavy knock on the door. My husband woke up startled:

'What's going on?'

I didn't wish to sadden him, so I replied:

'I don't know.'

But I was trembling with fear.

Believe me, one does not die of fright, for I survived that night.

My husband died the following day, which was a Saturday, at exactly ten o'clock."

(Told by an old flax-maker from Pluzunet).

- § -

The premonition of the corpse.

"I was about twelve years old. We lived in a little seaside hamlet where my father worked for the Customs. My mother had a brother, Uncle John, who lived not far away, where I sometimes spent Christmas or Easter with my cousins. I liked this uncle very much; he always brought me a souvenir from his travels, for he went far and wide as captain's mate on the Virginia, a ship from Nantes which sailed the South Seas. My mother was also very fond of her brother; he was a little younger than her, and she was his godmother. He wrote to her almost as often as to his wife, and, on the day I am speaking of, they had received a letter from him saying he had just reached Montivideo, that he was in good health, and that the Virginia would be setting sail for France.

Premonitions.

I remember these details very clearly because, as I have just said, I had a very lively interest in anything to do with my uncle.

We had dined alone, my mother and I; my father was out on coastguard duty. The weather was quite bad, with wind and rain mixed together. When it was time for me to go to bed, my mother said to me:

'At least don't forget Uncle John in your prayers.'

'There's no fear of that,' I replied.

I rarely failed to say a prayer especially for him, so that he would remember to bring me a nice present from the places he travelled to.

I did as usual that evening, but without being able to explain why, as I prayed I felt myself becoming sad, so sad that I ended up crying. Then my mother came over to my bed and said:

'What's making you cry like that? Go to sleep quickly; you know it's late.'

Whilst speaking to me like that, she pointed to a little dormer window, similar to a ship's porthole, which was set in the wall a little above my head, and through which one could see a square of the dark sky where the clouds passed. I dried my tears and pretended to close my eyes. But when my mother had gone back to her knitting near the table, I opened them again and stayed musing at the darkness. The wind blew in great gusts outside; but, in the calmer intervals I could hear the patter of the rain on the roof tiles. I could make out this noise all the better because our house had only one floor. Now, suddenly, it seemed to me that a drop of water had come through the attic floor and fallen on my bed-clothes. And after that, there was a second, then a third, then five, ten, twenty others, one after the other. It went tap, tap, tap, in little slow regular sounds. I called my mother.

'What?' she said. 'What is it now?'

'I think it's raining in on my bed.'

'What an idea!'

She ran her hand over my bed-clothes, took the candle to look at the ceiling, and ascertained that there was not the slightest sign of dampness anywhere. The noise had also stopped.

'You know I'll tell your father when he comes in, if you go on playing the fool and dreaming of things which aren't there instead of sleeping,' said my mother.

13

Premonitions.

I was afraid of my father who, although thoroughly good, was a rough-mannered man, and I promised to be as good as gold. However, my mother had scarcely settled down when the strange tap, tap, tap, started again. Despite all my efforts, I couldn't work out where this water which left no trace came from, and I must have fallen asleep in the end, for I didn't hear my father come in.

A sudden noise, like that of a dam bursting, woke me with a start. I sat up shivering, with my eyes wide open. What I saw then, froze me with such fear that I feel myself going pale when I think of it again after fifty years. The window - the one which was on the wall above my head - seemed to be shaking from a dreadful onslaught. It suddenly gave way and water gushed through the gaping hole. It came and it came. In the blinking of an eye, I felt myself submerged, and the water went up and up in green translucent layers. I thought I was sitting on the bottom of the sea. The wall, the ceiling, even the wood of my bed had all disappeared. Whichever way I looked, I could only see water, more water, water everywhere!... I believed myself to be someone who had drowned but had somehow stayed alive, and you can scarcely know how horrible it felt.

But the most terrifying thing about it was this:

When I was looking stupefied at the water piling up, the corpse of a half-naked man passed by, almost touching my face; it was stretched out and floating inert, moved about by the waves. Its arms were crossed, its legs apart. The remnants of a pair of red cloth pants were held by a length of rope around his waist!... I pushed myself violently backwards. My bed-clothes made a great deal of splashing. I thought they were going to carry me off with the corpse which they were dragging, and I made a heart-rending cry for help.

My father leapt to my bed in a single bound. I remember that he still had a gun in his hands which he was no doubt polishing, as he always did when he had been out in bad weather. He believed I was having a nightmare, and he shook me with all his might.

'Wake up, Marguerite!'

'I'm too much awake,' I replied.

My teeth were chattering and all my body was streaming with a cold sweat, just as if I really had come out of the water. My father spoke harshly:

'Well, what's taken you? What's happened to you? Speak!'

14

Premonitions.

I looked at him silently, with suppliant eyes. He softened his voice, caressed me, and encouraged me:

'Don't be afraid... Your mother's already told me that you've had strange ideas in your head; tell me what it is; I'll not shout at you.'

I threw my arms around his neck and began sobbing on his chest.

'The sea!' I exclaimed... 'It was all there in my bed, and there was a drowned man's body floating on it.'

'And what was this drowned man like?'

'I don't know... I only saw him from below, and I only noticed one thing, that he was wearing red pants like Uncle John's.'

'Well then, little one, it's a sign that Uncle John's in good health. Haven't you heard tell that one always dreams the opposite of the truth?'

'It wasn't a dream,' I murmured.

He didn't seem to understand.

'Give me your hand and go back to sleep. I'll stay by your side. That way you'll feel safe, won't you?'

'Yes, father.'

After a quarter of an hour, seeing that I no longer moved, he left me, thinking I was sound asleep, and went back to my mother. I heard her ask him softly:

'What do you think, Yvon?'

'I think your brother's dead. He's chosen to manifest himself to our child because he was very fond of her. She's just seen the premonition of his death.'

'My poor, poor brother! God has his soul!' said my mother, all pale.

And I saw her tears falling like rain over the work she was holding.

Twelve days later a dispatch arrived from Nantes, announcing on behalf of the company my uncle sailed for, that a transatlantic ship had come across an empty lifeboat recognised as belonging to the Virginia. As for the ship herself, they knew nothing. She must have struck a reef and gone straight down with all hands."

(Told by Marguerite Guerneur, Quimper).

- § -

15

Premonitions.

The reflection in the water.

"I was quite young then, but my memory of it is so clear that it could have happened yesterday. I'm sixty-eight now. I was scarcely twelve at the time I am speaking of. I had been taken on at a farm, through charity, to look after the cattle. That morning, they had sent me to pasture the herd by the river, from where the hay had been removed the previous day.

Whilst my animals were grazing here and there, I sat down on the river bank, and, to pass the time, I amused myself by striking the water with the stick I used for keeping them together.

Suddenly, I was startled.

Before me, in the water, which at that spot was still and clear, I could see the face and upper half of my master's body. It was just as clear as I see you now.

I even noticed that he looked sombre. I thought he was about to tell me off, because he had caught me lounging about like that, and I didn't dare look round.

My embarrassment lasted a good two or three minutes.

At last, surprised to receive neither a telling off nor a slap - for he was reputed to act promptly - I took courage and leapt up in a single bound.

Judge my stupefaction when I found there were only my cattle and I in the field.

Short of having been swallowed up by the earth, he could not have disappeared so quickly. On the other hand, there was no shadow of a doubt; it was clearly his reflection that I had just seen in the water.

I ruminated over this adventure all day long.

I returned with my animals at dusk. The first person I met, on opening the farm gate, was precisely the master.

'He said nothing to me back there,' I thought, 'but he's going to be rough with me now.'

Not at all! He greeted me, on the contrary, with kind words, went into the cow-shed with me and gently showed me how to tether the animals, something I hadn't been doing very well up till then.

Seeing he was in such good humour, I began to chat:

'You must have been quite hot today when you passed by the fields. You should have done like me and soaked your feet in the water. It refreshes the blood.'

'What's that you're saying?' he said. 'I haven't been near

the fields. It's market-day today, and I've just come back.'

It was only then that I noticed he was wearing his Sunday clothes.

'Well... I thought... It seemed like..,' I mumbled uneasily.

Fortunately the horn sounded for supper.

I didn't speak a word during supper, but I can assure you that my mind was tormented.

I shared a bed with the chief servant. It was at the end of the kitchen. When we were between the sheets, I said:

'There's evil hanging over this house.'

I told her my story. She treated me as though I were being foolish, but I saw clearly that she was no more reassured than I.

Before daybreak, before the cocks had crowed, I heard them calling for the chief servant, from near the master's bed at the other end of the kitchen. I dug my elbow into her, and she got up. She ran back shortly afterwards to tell me that the master had just died. I learnt later that he had died from a stroke."

(Told by a travelling fruit-seller, Quimper, 1888.)

- § -

The bullocks.

"This happened a little before the Revolution. I was told it by my mother, who was sixteen at the time; she never lied.

She was a cowherd on a farm near Briec. I can't tell you the exact name of the farm, but it was near the edge of the plain. I remember that the master was called Evan. He was a fine man, and what's more, a learned man. He had studied at college to become a priest, but he had preferred to return to farming, no doubt because he did not feel the priesthood to be his vocation. He had not forgotten what he had been taught in his youth, and he was highly regarded in the country, seeing that he could read all kinds of books. They even said he could speak in no matter what language with no matter whom.

One morning, he said to the carter:

'Yoke the youngest pair of bullocks, so that I can go and sell them at the market.'

He was like that. When it was a matter of buying or selling, he never decided until the last minute, and he always did well. They said he had a familiar spirit which whispered what he should do in his ear, just at the right moment.

The carter yoked the two youngest bullocks, and saddled a horse for the master.

The latter set out, after having given everyone their tasks for the day.

His wife, who had come to the door to watch him set off, said to my mother:

'As sure as the day's long, Tina, my man will bring me six hundred francs for those two young bullocks.'

My mother took her cows to the fields. She started to bring them back at dusk. The path she had to follow crossed the main highway, and, when she reached the crossing, she met the master on his way back from the market. She was more than surprised to see him returning with the pair of bullocks he had intended to sell. You know how in Lower Brittany they don't restrain themselves from chatting freely even with the masters:

'It seems to me,' said my mother, 'that the market has hardly given you anyhthing.'

'That's where you're wrong,' replied the master in a strange voice; 'it's given me more than I wished for.'

'Nay,' thought my mother... But whatever the case, he didn't look happy; he let his horse go by itself, the reins hanging over its neck. As for himself, he had his hands crossed and his head was hanging and thoughtful. The bullocks were escorting him with a kind of solmenity, one on the right, the other on the left; they must have lost their yoke at the market. Although young, they were two good, docile animals. They hadn't yet been harnessed to a plough, nor a cart, because Evan had reserved them for selling, but one could see from the peaceful way they walked with their muzzles near the ground, that they were quite ready for real work.

For the time being, they also seemed to be dreaming of sad things, like their master.

They walked for a while in silence, the cows in front. My mother wondered what the master had meant about the market giving him more than he had wished for.

He kept in the middle of the road, with the pair of bullocks. My mother went along the grass by the ditch.

Suddenly, Evan stopped her:

'Tina,' he said, 'I'll take the cows back myself. You take

this path and run to town like the wind. Go first to the carpenter's and order a coffin six feet long and two feet wide. Then go to the presbytery, and, whatever the priest is doing, beg him to bring his bag of extreme unction and follow you back home as quickly as possible.'

My mother looked at the master, stupefied. Tears were rolling down his cheeks.

'Go,' he said, 'and be quick about it.'

My mother held her clogs in her hands, took the path, and ran to town like the wind.

She was back at the farm an hour later, accompanied by a priest.

The farmer's wife was sitting on the doorstep:

'You're too late,' said the latter to the priest, 'my husband is dead.'

My mother couldn't believe her ears.

The farmer's wife asked the priest inside. My mother slipped in behind them, into the kitchen. They had lain a mattress on the table, and the master was laid out on it, dead. He was still dressed in his daily clothes. The priest sprinkled the corpse with holy water and began the prayers for the dead.

When he had left, my mother was sent to bed, because they were going to prepare for washing the corpse.

Her bed was at the lower end of the house, separated from the kitchen by a simple planked partition. There's no need to tell you that my mother didn't feel like sleeping. She made a semblance of going to bed, pulling the blankets over her, but, after a little while, she got up in her nightshirt and glued her ear to the partition.

Only Evan's widow and two neighbouring old women, who usually helped on such occasions, remained in the kitchen.

In the yard, one could hear the people of the house, and others from the surroundings who had come for the wake. They were all asking one another how such a hefty man had come to die so suddenly.

That was also the question which intrigued my mother. She soon learnt the answer, for she didn't miss a word the farmer's wife said to the two old women in the kitchen, whilst they were washing Evan's body together.

'You know,' said the farmer's wife, 'that he never missed selling anything. When I saw him coming back with the two bullocks, I reproached him with it.

"Evan," I said, "this time you've failed."

19

Premonitions.

"It's the first time, and it will be the last," he replied.

"Hope to God it is," said I.

He looked at me strangely, and said:

"There's a wish you'll soon regret to see granted, for it will bring you great pain..... Yes," he went on, after a pause, "it's the first time you can find fault with one of my dealings, and it will also be the last, because I'll never go to market again in my life. They will bury me tomorrow."

I wanted to believe he was not serious, but I remembered something he had said repeatedly, not long before: "I shall be the first to be warned of my death." When I saw how upset he was, fear seized hold of me. Clearly he must have had his premonition. Trembling, I asked him:

"What's happened since this morning?"

"My God," he said, "we had reached the place where the road goes down, when the bullocks, which until then had gone along peacefully, suddenly stopped and set themselves to bellowing. Then one of them said to the other, in animal language: 'Are we being taken to town?' 'Yes,' replied the other, 'but we will be brought back to the plain this evening.' I showed them in the market. The people started going around them, each one saying, 'what a fine pair of steers,' but no one asked me the price. It was like that all day long. For a long time I controlled my impatience, but when I saw everyone going and the night drawing in, I could no longer prevent myself from swearing and cursing. To tell the truth, I think that right then I would have given my two beasts for nothing, if I had found a taker. The grey and black bullock had started pawing the ground with its hoof, so I gave it a kick in the belly. Then it looked at me sadly from the corner of its eye, and said: 'Evan, it will be dark within two hours, and in four hours time you will be dead. Let's go back to the farm, quickly, so that you can put your conscience in order, and so that we can prepare for our work tomorrow, which will be to draw you to your burial.' " '

'That's what my husband told me,' added the farmer's wife; 'anyone else would have gone into a rage with the bullock, but he, being a sensible man, followed the bullock's advice. Thanks to it he died, not in the roadside ditch, like an animal, but in his home, provisioned for his journey with a priest's prayers, like a good Christian.'

'God pardon the dead,' murmured the two old women.

My mother made the sign of the cross, and went back to bed.

Premonitions.

The next day, the two bullocks pulled the funeral cart to town.

This took place a little before the Revolution. Since that time, they say that cattle no longer speak, except perhaps at midnight on Christmas Eve."

(Told by an old fruit-seller, Quimper, 1887.)

- § -

The pond.

"John was a good worker during the week, but on a Sunday it was a miracle if he didn't stay out till late in the night, drinking pints in the inns of a nearby town. Most often, they had to dine without him, and sometimes they were still waiting for him after they had washed the dishes. Then his wife would say to her daughter:

'Put your coat on and go and fetch your drunkard of a father; if you don't do so, he might be legless and drown himself in the pond.'

There was a deep pond by the roadside, in an old disused quarry. And that is why the girl only obeyed reluctantly. She dreaded having to go past this great hole full of water, where they said one could 'see the things of the night' and 'hear terrifying noises.'

She would go all the same, for otherwise her mother would have beaten her; and then, she was very fond of her father who was kind to her and not too much trouble when she was sent to bring him back home.

Now, on the night of which we are speaking, it was full moon and the surface of the pond, which was usually black, was shining like polished silver. Because of this, instead of turning her head the other way as she usually did, the girl cast a glance across the water. She was highly surprised to see a laundress on the other side, on her knees and with her sleeves rolled up, about to do some washing. The girl could not make out her features, but as her hair-style and dress were like the local peasants', she had not doubt that it was someone from the parish. She had the courage to speak to her in the usual way:

'It looks like you're washing,' she said.

'Yes,' she replied, and she called her by her own name, as though she knew her.

'You've chosen a strange day and a strange time,' said

21

the girl, feeling more confident.

The woman replied:

'In our work, we've no choice.'

'Then it must be an urgent task?'

'Yes, for it's the sheet which will be used tomorrow to shroud the one you're going to fetch.'

And, on saying that, the woman held up a shroud which increased in size until it covered the whole pond. The girl ran away, terrified. She arrived, out of breath, at the door of the inn her father used to call his 'last station,' after the stations of the cross. She believed she was going to find him dead, and she was quite relieved to find him not much drunker than usual. She took him with her, half-dragging, half-holding him up. When they reached the pond there was no sign of the laundress nor the shroud. She thought:

'I bet it must have been a neighbour. She would have been annoyed at having been caught washing on a Sunday, at a time when she had hoped no one would have been about. She must have been afraid that I would recognise her, and told me terrifying things to frighten me away.'

Therefore she did not tell her father about it, nor her mother, who was in bed when they got back. She went to bed with her mind at rest, whilst the drunkard installed himself, as was his custom, in a corner by the fire to eat the supper they had left keeping warm there. What happened then? God alone knows. His wife woke up during the night and realised he had not come to bed. She called out loud to him, thinking he had fallen asleep by the hearth. As he did not reply, she got up to shake him. By the light of the candle he had left burning, she saw that the bowl between his knees was still half-full. He was sleeping, but it was the sleep of those who are no longer hungry nor thirsty; of the last sleep. God pardon the dead."

(Told by Jean-Pierre Dupont, Quimper.)

Chapter 2. Before death.

Dead man's treasure.

"There was a farmer's wife who saw a man by the gate to the road, every time she went into her yard. The man was a local who had been dead for almost five years. He made signs to her with his hand, as though he were inviting her to follow him somewhere. One fine day, when she was fed up with her housework, she was bold enough to walk up to him and say:

'What's all this about? What do you want of me?'

He made a sign for her to go through the gateway and follow him.

'O dear!' she said to herself; 'anyway, I'll have this cleared up once and for all.'

And off she went following the dead man's footsteps. He took her to the top of an empty heath, where there was a great rock. The man knelt on the ground and began scraping away the earth with his fingers. When he had finished, he turned towards the woman and showed her the hole he had just dug. She leant over and saw a heap of golden coins which shone like new. Never before had she seen such a sum. Whilst she was looking at the gold with a mixture of admiration and envy, the dead man disappeared.

'If he's shown me his hiding place, no doubt it's so that I can benefit from what it contains,' she thought.

And, picking the coins up by the handful, she filled her apron. Back home, she piled them up in her cupboard. In the evening, she said to her husband:

'If you'd like a new horse, you can buy not just one, but four, ten, or more; for we're rich.'

'How's that come about?' he asked, all happy.

She told him her adventure, but her husband's face darkened.

'If you value your life, go quickly and put this money back where you found it.'

'Why?'

'Because if you don't get rid of it, you'll surely die within a year.'

As soon as it was morning, she ran to the top of the heath and put the gold coins back in their place. But when, a few days later, she went to take some linen out of her cupboard, she heard the sound of money; she looked and was stupefied when she saw that all the dead man's treasure had come back to her.

23

Before death.

'That's just what I feared,' said her husband. 'You should go and find the priest; perhaps he could give you some good advice.'

But the priest stopped her after the first few words of her story.

'There's nothing I can do for you,' he said. 'You've delivered this dead man, and now you must soon take his place. You should prepare yourself to die like a Christian, and stipulate in your will that they put the treasure in your coffin. Only by doing that can you be saved.'

It was not long before she died, and without having been ill. And they buried her with the dead man's treasure so that it would harm no one else."

(Told by Perrine Laz, Quimper.)

- § -

The woman and the two dogs.

"This happened at the time when the linen cloths of Lower Brittany were the most renowned of all. There was not a spinner in the land who could spin as fine as Fant Ar Merrer. She went to market every Wednesday to sell her yarn. One Tuesday night, she said to herself:

'I must be up early tomorrow.'

She went to bed with this on her mind.

She woke up in the middle of the night, and was surprised to find it was almost daylight. She got up and dressed in great haste, threw her bundle of yarn over her shoulders, and set out.

When she reached the road which goes to the Cross of Brabant, she met a young man.

They greeted each other and walked side by side as far as the cross.

There, the young man took hold of Fant Ar Merrer by the arm, and said to her:

'Let's stop here.'

He pushed her into the ditch, against the bank, and placed himself in front of her as though to protect her.

Almost as soon as they had reached the side of the road, she heard a terrifying noise approaching. Never had she heard such a din. If there had been a hundred heavy wagons rolling at a gallop, they could not have made so much noise.

The noise came closer and closer.

Before death.

Fant was trembling all over. Nevertheless, she tried to see what it could be.

A woman passed by on the road, running like the wind; she went so fast that the wings of her hat were flapping as though they were birds' wings. Her bare feet scarcely touched the ground, and drops of blood were falling from them. Her untied hair flowed behind her. She waved her arms in gestures of despair, and cried pitifully.

Her cries were so agonising that Fant Ar Merrer went cold all over, right down to her toes.

This woman was followed by two dogs which seemed to be disputing over which one should devour her.

One of these dogs was black, the other white.

It was they who were making all the din.

The bowels of the earth resounded with every bound they made.

The woman fled towards the cross.

Fant Ar Merrer saw her throw herself on the steps of the cross. Just then, the black dog managed to bite on the end of her skirt; but she threw herself forward, hugging the base of the cross and holding on with all her might.

The black dog disappeared there and then, letting out a terrible howl.

The white dog was left alone, close to the unhappy one, and it began licking her wounds.

Then the young man said to Fant Ar Merrer:

'Now you can go on your way. It's only midnight. Don't risk exposing yourself again to seeing what you've just seen. I'll not always be there to protect you. There are times when one should not be out on the roads. When you reach Kervénou, go into the house. You'll find a dying man there. Spend the rest of the night at his bedside, reciting the prayers for the dying, and don't leave until dawn. As for me, I'm your guardian angel.' "

(Told by Marie-Louise Bellec, Port-Blanc.)

Chapter 3. The Ankou.

The Ankou is death personified, the worker of death, or 'Father Time.'

- § -

In many places, the last one to die in each year becomes the Ankou; in a few places, it is the first one to die.

When there have been more deaths than usual in a year, they say the Ankou is a wicked one.

Sometimes they depict the Ankou as a tall, thin man with long white hair and a face shaded by a large felt hat; sometimes in the form of a skeleton draped in a shroud, and whose head turns continuously, just like a weather cock, so that he can see all the region he has to cover at a single glance.

In the one case or the other, he holds a scythe. The latter differs from ordinary scythes in having its blade turned the other way round, so that when he uses it, instead of bringing it towards him, he pushes it forwards.

- § -

The Ankou's coach is similar to the ones they used in the old days for transporting the dead.

It is usually pulled by two horses harnessed in line. The one in front is thin, emaciated, and scarcely able to stand on its feet. The one behind is fat, with a shiny coat, and without a collar.

The Ankou stands in the coach.

He is escorted by two companions, both of whom walk. One of them leads the first horse by the bridle. The other has the job of opening field gates, and the doors of houses. He is also the one who piles the dead up in the coach; the dead whom the Ankou has harvested.

- § -

When the Ankou sets out on his tour, they say his coach is filled with pebbles so that it will go heavily, making more noise.

When he reaches a house where there is someone whom he must harvest, he abruptly discharges his load, to make room for his new 'ballast.'

That is the cause of the sound of pebbles which is heard

so often in homes where they are watching over a dying person, just at the time of the latter's last breath.

- § -

The coach of the dead.

"It was a night in June, at the time when they leave the horses out all night.

A young man had taken his horses to the fields. He was whistling on his way back, for the night was clear and the moon was shining. He heard a coach coming towards him on the road; a coach whose badly-greased axle went squeak, squeak.

He was sure it was the coach of death.

'At last I'll be able to see that coach with my own eyes,' he thought.

And he crossed the ditch and hid himself in a clump of hazels, so that he could see without being seen.

The coach came into view.

It was drawn by three white horses harnessed one behind the other. Two men accompanied it, both of them dressed in black and wearing wide-brimmed felt hats. One of them led the first horse by the bridle, the other was standing up in the front of the coach.

As the coach came opposite the hazel clump where the young man was hiding, its axle went 'crack.'

'Stop!' said the man on the coach, to the one who was leading the horses.

The latter cried: 'Whoa!' and the team came to a halt.

'The axle pin's just broken,' said the Ankou. 'Go and cut what you need to make a new one from that hazel clump over there.'

'I'm lost,' thought the young man, who right then regretted his indiscreet curiosity very much.

However, he was not punished there and then. The coachman cut off a branch, shaped it, inserted it into the axle, and then the horses continued on their way.

The young man was able to return home safe and sound, but, towards morning, he was taken with an unknown fever, and they buried him the next day."

(Told by Francoise, daughter of Jeanne Le Gac, 1890.)

- § -

The Ankou.

Gab Lucas.

"Gab Lucas worked at Rune-Riou. He went back every night to Kerdrenkenn where he lived with his wife Madelaine and five children, in the most miserable thatched cottage of that poor village. For Gab Lucas had only the ten pennies that he earned by very hard work each day. This did not prevent him from having a happy nature and being a good worker. The owners of Rune-Riou valued him. At the end of the week, they often invited him to spend Saturday evening with them, drinking flip* and eating roast chestnuts. At the stroke of ten the farmer would give Gab his weekly wage and his wife would always add some present for the household at Kerdrenkenn.

One Saturday night, she said to him:

'Gab, I've put a sack of potatoes aside for you. Give them to Madelaine on my behalf.'

Gab Lucas thanked her, threw the sack on his back, and set off home, after having wished everyone good night.

It is a good three-quarters of a league from Rune-Riou to Kerdrenkenn. Gab walked sprightly at first. The moon was shining, and the good flip he had drunk warmed his stomach. He whistled a Breton air to keep himself company, happy that Madelaine would be pleased when she saw him return with a good sack of potatoes. They would cook a large potful the next day; they would add a slice of pork belly to it, and they would all enjoy themselves.

All went well for a quarter of a league.

But then the virtue of the flip wore off in the coolness of the night. Gab felt all the tiredness of the day's work come back to him. The sack of potatoes began to weigh heavy on his shoulders. Soon, he no longer felt like whistling.

'If only a wagon would come by,' he thought... 'But I'll have no such luck.'

Just then he reached the cross where the track from the farm at Nizilzi joins the road.

'Well,' said Gab, 'I can always sit on the steps of the cross for a moment, whilst I catch my breath.'

He set his load down, sat beside it, and lit his pipe.

The countryside was silent all around.

Suddenly, the dogs of Nizilzi began to howl pitifully.

'Why on earth are they making such a din?' wondered Gab

*A drink made from rum and cider.

28

Then he heard the sound of a cart coming along the road from Nizilzi. Its badly-greased axle went squeak, squeak.

'It looks,' said Gab to himself, 'as though my wish is about to come true. They must be going for a load of sand. They'll take my sack right to my door.'

He saw the horses come into view, and then the cart. They were terribly thin and emaciated, those horses. They were certainly not from Nizilzi, because their horses were always so fat and shiny. As for the cart, its base was made of a few loosely-fitted planks; two rude hurdles served as sides. A great gawk of a man, who was just as scraggy as his beasts, led this pitiful team. A large felt hat shaded all his face. Gab could not recognise him. He greeted him all the same:

'Comrade, would you have room for this sack in your cart? My back's aching. I'm only going as far as Kerdrenkenn.'

The carter did not reply.

'He must not have heard me,' said Gab to himself. 'That awful cart of his makes such a noise.'

The opportunity was too good to be missed. Gab hurredly put his pipe out, stuffed it in his jacket pocket, grabbed the sack of potatoes, and ran after the cart, which was going fast enough. He ended by catching up with it, and dropped his sack inside, letting out a sigh of relief.

But, how do you explain that? The sack went through the old planks and landed on the ground.

'What sort of a cart is this?' said Gab to himself.

He picked up his sack, and once more put it in the cart, but this time further forward.

But the base of the cart had no solidity, for the sack and Gab went through it. Both of them rolled on the ground.

The strange team continued on its way. Its mysterious leader had not even turned his head.

Gab let them move away from him. When they had disappeared, he took his own turn to go up to Kerdrenkenn, where he arrived half-dead from fright.

'What's wrong?' asked Madelaine, seeing him so upset.

Gab told her his adventure.

'It's quite simple,' said his wife to him. 'You've met the coach of the dead.'

Gab almost had a fit. The next day, they heard the church bell ringing. The Master of Nizilzi had died on the previous night, towards half-past ten."

(Told by Marie-Yvonne Mainguy, Port-Blanc.)

29

Chapter 4. Simulated death.

Don't play with death.

"Liza, of Kerevénou manor, was the prettiest peasant girl of the whole region.

She had been engaged for several months to Loll ar Briz, a young man who came to see her every Sunday.

Liza was a gay and fun-loving person. Loll loved her in a way which was too serious for her liking; she would often tease him, and the pranks she enjoyed playing on him sometimes went beyond a joke.

There was a little servant at the manor who was at least as mischievous as Liza. She helped her mistress to tease poor Loll. When the latter would come to the manor on a Sunday morning, Liza would rarely be there to greet him. The little servant would take it on herself to explain his sweetheart's absence, spinning him a highly improbable yarn. Liza, in fact, would simply have gone to hide in the attic, or behind the pile of straw in the yard. She would suddenly show herself, just as Loll was about to retrace his steps and return home. Then the two silly girls would burst out laughing. Loll would soon cheer himself up, whilst reproaching his loved one for childishly wasting time that could have been so well spent saying sweet things to each other.

But Liza was incorrigible.

One Saturday night, she said to the little servant with whom she slept:

'What silly trick should we play on Loll ar Briz tomorrow?'

'Lady,' replied the little servant, 'whatever we do, it must be something new, for almost all our old tricks have gone stale.'

'That's my opinion, too. Listen, Annie (that was the little servant's name), I've got an idea. I'd like to find out if Loll loves me as much as he says. When he comes tomorrow and asks you where I am, you must look very sad and answer him as follows: "Alas! She's with God, and you'll never see her in this world again." '

'You're going to play dead, Liza?'

'Precisely.'

'They say it's not good to do that.'

'Bah! An innocent joke... Only to see if Loll would really be upset if he believed me dead.'

'All right,' replied Annie.

They spent a good half of the night organising the plot.

The sun rose on the next day. Our two silly girls went off

30

to early mass, as was their custom since Loll ar Briz had been allowed to come courting Liza. Then she could spend the time of the high mass alone with him, whilst all the others from the manor were in town. When the bells rang half an hour before the high mass, the older members of the family, the servants and the swine-herd, would all set off in the direction of the town. Only Liza and the little servant girl would remain in the house. That was the time Loll chose to make his appearance.

On the Sunday we are speaking of, as soon as they were alone, the two young girls hurried to put into effect the project they had planned the night before. Liza stretched herself out on the kitchen table, her head resting on a piece of bread which she had wrapped in a fresh napkin from the cupboard.

The little servant spread a sheet over Liza's body.

Then she went and sat on the narrow bench that ran the length of the kitchen wall.

The last peal of bells had just rung for the high mass. The sound of the bells had scarcely faded away when Loll ar Briz appeared in the open doorway.

'Good day and joy to you, Annie; where's Liza, your mistress?'

'It's bad day and sadness that you should be saying, Loll ar Briz,' said Annie the prankster, in a crying tone.

'Are you trying to say that she no longer loves me, or that since last Sunday someone's been here and taken my place?'

'Liza will not be your wife, nor anyone else's. Liza's with God now.'

'Dead! Liza!... Take care Annie. Not all jokes are good.'

'But look over at the table! Lift the sheet and see what's beneath it.'

The young peasant became quite pale, whilst the little servant was most amused, inside herself.

He went over and lifted the sheet, and drew back horrified.

'Alas, it's only too true,' he exclaimed.

'Loll,' said Annie keeping herself serious, 'haven't you heard them say that a lover can resuscitate his dead loved one by taking her on his knees and giving her a kiss? You should try this remedy.'

'What! You're still joking?'

'Try, I tell you, and don't be angry. Hold on, I'll help you.'

31

Simulated death.

She got up from the bench where she was sitting, but she had scarcely reached the table when she nearly fell over backwards.

Liza really had taken on the colour of death. Her wide-open eyes could no longer see.

'It's not possible! It's not possible!' cried Annie..... 'Here, Loll ar Briz; help me.... Let's sit her up.... I swear she's alive.... She can't be dead....'

Yes, Liza was dead, and quite dead. The united efforts of Annie and Loll ar Briz only served to torment a corpse.

They buried the pretty heiress of Kerevénou the next day, in the cemetery at Faouët.

Loll probably recovered from it, in the long run, but the little servant girl went mad."

(Told by Jeanne-Marie Toulouzan*, Port-Blanc.)

*'I worked in Faouët when this happened,' added Jean-Marie Toulouzan. 'I didn't know the people in the story, but local workers with whom I worked often met the poor mad girl. She went from house to house begging for food. She would suddenly burst out laughing, and, a moment later, she would cry enough to break one's heart.'

Chapter 5. Means of calling death on someone.

"One of the most infallible means of ridding youreself of an enemy, is to vow your hatred of the latter before Saint Yves-of-the-Truth.

You make Saint Yves the judge of the dispute.

But you must be quite sure that right is on your side; if you are the one in the wrong, you yourself will suffer."

- § -

The story of the farrier.

"Once there was a farrier who had a forge in the town. He cultivated several measures of land adjoining his forge, and he managed to keep two or three cows. He could have been quite well off, for he was a good worker. Unfortunately, his wife was a spendthrift. When Fanchi gave her money, he never saw it again, and he never knew where it had gone. He never knew, good man, that whilst he slaved over the anvil, his wife went from inn to inn paying for coffee laced with brandy for herself and all the old bibbers of the neighbourhood.

Fanchi had an apprentice called Louis, who had worked for him for many years and in whom he had great trust.

One evening, he said to his apprentice:

'Get up early tomorrow. My wife says her purse is empty. We'll go to market and sell the red cow; perhaps we'll get a good price for her.'

The red cow was, in fact, sold for a good price.

When Loius and Fanchi were on their way back, the apprentice said to the master:

'If I were in your place, I wouldn't give my wife all this money at once. I would keep it in a drawer, and from time to time take out enough for the housekeeping.'

'What a good idea,' replied Fanchi, who had never thought of anything like that before.

Back home, he locked the money in a large oak cupboard, and put the key under his bolster.

But his action had not escaped his wife's eyes. As soon as she heard her husband snoring after his tiring day, she got up quietly, stole the key, ran to the cupboard, and took the money.

Who was taken in the next day? It was Fanchi the farrier. His suspicions fell blindly on his apprentice.

'Louis,' he cried, white with anger, 'I followed your advice

and see what's happened to me. Give me my money back.'
'I didn't take it.'
'You deny it? So be it; your're coming with me to Saint Yves-of-the-Truth!'
'I'll go wherever you want.'
They set out.
When they reached the door of the oratory, the Farrier pronounced the sacred words. The saint nodded his head three times to show that he had understood, and also to indicate that he was going to give justice.
Fanchi returned home feeling better. As for Louis, he had been cheerful from the start, and was still the same when they got back.
On entering the town, Fanchi said to him:
'You realise that from now on we'll no longer be working together.'
'It's your wish, master,' replied Louis. 'I think, however, that before long you'll realise that I'm not the one who is guilty.'
They parted company.
The farrier's wife was looking out for him from the door-way of the forge.
'Where have you been?' she asked him.
'To Saint Yves-of-the-Truth.'
'What for?'
'To vow death within twelve months on the person who stole my money.'
'Ah! What misfortune! What unhappiness!' cried his wife, whose neck had already turned the colour of death; 'if only you had told me first! Your money hasn't been stolen. It was I who took it, last night whilst you were asleep. Let's go back and undo what you have done.'
'It's too late, woman. The saint has nodded his head three times.'
From that day on, his wife began to languish, and when the twelve months had gone by, she died."
(Told by Marie-Hyacinthe Toulouzan, Port-Blanc).

- § -

Means of calling death on someone.

The story of the gun.

"We had a lot of broom growing on a hillside, quite some distance from the house. There was no shortage of people who went and helped themselves without our permission, so my older brother decided one evening to go and keep watch in order to catch a thief. When he was about to leave, I saw him going towards the mantelpiece (where the gun was hanging).

'Goodness gracious,' I said to him, 'don't take the gun.'

But he wouldn't listen to me.

An hour later he came back, full of anger.

'What's wrong?'

'They've not only stolen our broom, but they've taken my gun as well.'

And he told us how, just as he had climbed up the slope to the broom, with his gun in his hand, someone who had been hiding had grabbed it by the barrel, wrenched it from his grasp, and run off with it.

'And didn't you see who it was?' asked my father.

'Yes I did; I clearly recognised him. It was Hervé Bideau, the harness maker.

'Oh! He's a bad lot... You can say goodbye to your gun, for you'll never see it again.'

'Why not?.... I'll have it back tomorrow morning, by fair means or foul.'

'No, because the harness maker will take it to the Town Hall, saying that he found you hunting with it in the close season. You'll be prosecuted and fined, and the judges will confiscate your gun.'

'Haven't we the right to protect ourselves from thieves?'

'How can you prove that he stole it. Where are your witnesses?'

'A curse of God!' exclaimed my brother. 'I'll not ask for my gun back, but if Bideau hasn't returned it by the same time tomorrow evening, as sure as I'm standing here, I'll go and vow him to Saint Yves.'

'Don't talk like that,' said my father, 'you don't know what you're letting yourself in for.'

'So much the worse! I'll not let it drop. They've got to learn where right and truth lie.'

We hoped that he would calm down after a night's sleep, but as soon as it was morning, he was on his feet, just as angry as the night before.

Means of calling death on someone.

'Where are you going?'

'To look for Anna Rouz.'

This Anna Rouz was an old pilgrim who knew all possible prayers for giving life to people, and also for taking it away from them. She lived not far from us, in a sort of mud and straw hut where people went to consult her at any time of the day or night. My brother went there and invited her, as was the custom when one required her help, to come and have supper with us that same evening. He came back calmer, told us that the old woman would be coming at dusk, and went off to work in the fields. But as for my father, he was still troubled:

'If Evan however' - Evan was my brother's name - 'what if Evan hasn't the right on his side....,' he kept repeating.

In the end, being no longer able to sit still, he decided to profit from my brother's absence, by trying to persuade the harness maker to return the gun himself. He went off to town to find him.

'Listen,' he said, 'Evan has decided to take matters further. If you don't put things right, he's going to vow Saint Yves-of-the-Truth to pronounce the sentence.'

'I don't care about Saint Yves, your son, nor you,' replied the insolent harness maker.

'If something bad happens to you, you'll only have yourself to blame,' said my father.

And he came back home and told me how his proposal had been received.

'Don't say anything of this to your brother,' he said to me. 'We'll just have to let things sort themselves out.'

At the end of the day, as our people were coming back from their work, we saw Anna Rouz coming. She had put her Sunday clothes on, and was wearing her walking shoes, which were mens', and of a large size. She sat down with us at the table and, when the meal was over, waited until the servants had left the kitchen before speaking about why my brother had called on her.

'Well,' she said, addressing herself to my father, 'do you agree that I should go to Saint Yves-of-the-Truth on your son's behalf?'

'Yes,' replied my father, lowering his head.

'And you, Evan,' she went on, turning towards my brother, 'are you still determined to run the risk?'

'More than ever!' he declared in a firm voice. 'Saint Yves must pronounce in favour of him or me.'

36

Means of calling death on someone.

'Then say the following after me:

> Otro sant Erwan ar Wirioné
> A var deus an eil hag eguilé,
> Laket ar gwir elec'h ma man,
> Hag an tort gant an hini man ganthan.'

(My lord Saint Yves-of-the-Truth - who knows the for and against - put the right where it should be - and the wrong with whom it should be).

My father and I both went cold all over; but my brother repeated all of it, after the old woman, without trembling.

'Good,' she said. 'Now you must obtain two things for me: First, an eighteen denier piece, and second a handful of nails which haven't been counted.'

At that time, they generally kept all sorts of old money in the house; money which was no longer in circulation, but which, they said, brought happiness. My father went to his cupboard, took out a little boot full of old coins, and found the one that Anna Rouz had asked for; then, going to the far end of the house, he closed his eyes and took a handful of nails from a chest where all sorts of bits of iron were kept.

'Here you are,' he said, handing it all to the 'vower.'

She wet her finger with saliva and traced a cross on the coin, before slipping it in her bodice; as for the handful of nails, she made it disappear in one of her apron pockets.

'Without being too inquisitive, Anna,' said my father, 'can you tell us how you go about it?'

'I've nothing to hide,' she replied, 'since it's for you that I'm working. Tomorrow morning, as soon as the cock crows, after having stayed awake all night fully dressed, I shall go first of all to the parish church where I shall make a short prayer, then I shall make a brief stop in front of Hervé Bideau's door, where I shall cross myself three times with my left hand; only after that shall I set out, taking care not to speak to anyone, not even replying to a greeting, until I'm out of sight of our belfry. On the way I shall have to stop at three crossroads, making three signs of the cross at each one, always with the left hand. Once at Tréguier, I shall wait for sunset before going to the chapel on the other side. If there's no one about, I shall approach the unglazed window in the gable and throw the handful of nails inside. I shall then go three times round the Saint's house, going in

37

the opposite direction to the sun, as they do with the dead, and say three *De profundis* for the deliverance of abandoned souls. Then I shall go inside, place the coin on the altar at the saint's feet, and say: "You know why and for whom I have come; you are paid; do justice." That's all; now you know as much as I do.'

'Yes,' murmured my father, 'but all the same, it's a dreadful thing.'

'If, for one reason or another, you should change your mind during the night, you'll still be able to withdraw any time before the cock crows.'

Anna Rouz thereupon wished us good night, and went back home. My brother also went off to the stable, where he slept. I myself went to bed, but my father stayed up alone, by candle light, thinking in front of the hot embers. He was very sad. I couldn't sleep, and I could see, through a gap in the panels of my closed bed, that he had his head in his hands and he was weeping. I wanted to console him, but I was just as heartbroken as he was, and I could think of nothing to say. Suddenly, I thought I heard someone walking across the mud in the yard. Then I called out:

'Father!'

'What is it, my girl?'

'There's someone outside.'

He stood up, went and removed the bar which locked the door, opened it and said:

'Is that you, Evan?'

'No,' replied a voice, 'It's me, Hervé Bideau the harness maker.... I behaved badly towards you this morning; I was in the wrong; I've come to make peace and return the gun.'

'Come in,' said my father.

'I breathed a sigh of relief; it was as though a great weight had been lifted off my chest. My father fetched a pitcher of cider and the two men drank to one another's health like friends. When Bideau was ready to take his leave, my father said to him:

'Wait a moment; I'm coming with you; I must call in on Anna Rouz.'

And he took two gold coins to pay the old woman, for this kind of work had to be paid for even when it was cancelled."

(Told by Marie-Anne Prigent, Pédernec, 1894.)

Chapter 6. The departure of the soul.

The soul seen in the form of a white mouse.

"Although Ludo Garel was only a servant, he was far from stupid. His mind was continually occupied with many things that the common people never think about. His continual meditations had taken him very far. He claimed that he knew almost everything it was given for man to know.

He would always add:'There is still a point which embarrasses me and on which I have seen no light; the separation of the soul from the body. When I shall have cleared up this point, there'll be nothing left for me to learn.'

His master, one of the last of the noble House of Quinquez, had great confidence in him, looking on him as a man of honour and a good adviser.

One fine day, he called him to his room.

'My poor Ludo,' he said, 'I'm not at my best today. I think I'm incubating some serious illness, and I've a premonition that I'll not escape from it. If only my affairs were in order! That accursed lawsuit in Rennes is tormenting me. It's been dragging on for nearly two years. At least if I could see it settled in my favour, before dying, I could go with a lighter heart. I look on you as a sensible person, Ludo, and, as you've proved in the past, there's nothing you wouldn't do for me. I'm asking you this, and it will probably be the last thing I shall ask you. Tomorrow morning, at the crack of dawn, set out for Rennes. Go and see each of the judges and ask them each to pronounce as soon as possible for, or against me. You have a sweet tongue; I can count on you finding a way to dispose them in my favour. As for me, I'm going to put myself to bed. I hope God will not take me from this world before you come back!'

Before taking his leave, Ludo tried to raise his master's fallen spirits.

'You should only think about getting back on your feet. You're not yet ripe for death. I trust I'll find you better when I return. I'll see to the rest, I assure you!'

He spent the afternoon preparing for his journey and in chewing over in his mind how he would speak to the judges.

He went to bed at dusk, so as to be awake as early as possible. He slept badly. A thousand ideas, a thousand incoherent propositions rushed around his head.

Suddenly, he thought he heard a cock crow.

'Ha, ha!' he said to himself, 'it's daybreak; time to go.'

And Ludo set off.

The departure of the soul.

It was mid-winter. He could scarcely see to walk. After an hour or so he found himself at the foot of a wall which blocked his way. He went along it and came to some stone steps which he climbed one after the other. It was the stairway to a cemetery.

'Hmm,' thought Ludo, when he saw himself surrounded by tombstones and crosses, 'I'm glad it's long past the evil hour!'

He had not finished talking to himself like that, when he saw a shadow fall on the ground and move towards him along one of the side-paths. When the shadow was quite close, Ludo saw that it came from a distinguished-looking young man who was dressed in fine black cloth.

He greeted the man.

'Good day,' replied the latter. 'You're travelling early.'

'I don't know exactly what time it is, but the cock was crowing when I left the house.'

'Yes, the white cock*!' replied the young man. 'Which way are you going?'

'I'm going towards Rennes.'

'So am I. We can go part of the way together, if you like.'

'I could ask for nothing better.'

The young man's voice and expression inspired confidence. Ludo Garel, a little wary at first, was soon delighted to have him as his companion, especially as the day was such a long time in coming. They chatted on the way. Ludo became more and more talkative. He told the unknown one from the cemetery everything about himself, all about his master's mysterious illness, the forebodings the latter had expressed the day before, and the reason for his journey. The unknown one listened, and said next to nothing.

Then the cock crowed on a nearby farm.

'Dawn's about to break!' exclaimed Ludo.

'Not yet,' replied the young man. 'That was a grey cock.'

Time went by, and the night stayed dark.

Our people went on walking; but Ludo had told all his secrets, and the unknown one did not seem inclined to tell his own. The conversation tailed-off, and finally ended.

When one doesn't chat during the day, one is bored; at night, one is afraid**.

---

*White and grey cocks, said the storyteller, are hare-brained; they cannot judge the time, and one should not trust their crowing.

**I should point out that my storyteller is a woman.

The departure of the soul.

Ludo Garel began to look at his companion out of the corner of his eye and found his demeanour quite strange. He
wished for daybreak with all his might.

At last, a third cock crowed.

'Ah!' said Ludo, with a sigh of relief; 'this time it's a
good one.'

'Yes,' replied the young man, 'it's a red one. Now dawn is
going to lighten the sky; but you'll find you've gone further
than you think. It was scarcely midnight when you went into
the cemetery where you met me.'

'That's possible,' said Ludo in a low voice.

'In future, try to be sure of the time. If I hadn't been with
you until now, you'd have had more than one unpleasant adventure.'

'Many thanks, then,' Ludo murmured humbly.

'That's not all. I have to tell you that there's no need for
you to continue on your journey. Your master's lawsuit was
judged yesterday evening in his favour. You should go back
and tell him this good news.'

'Fantastic! The count will be cured when he hears it.'

'No. On the contrary, he's going to die. And with regard
to that, Ludo Garel, you shall be permitted to see the separation of the soul from the body. It's something that I
know you've been longing to see.'

'Did I tell you that?' exclaimed Ludo who was asking himself, a little too late, if he hadn't said too much along the
way.

'You didn't tell me; but he who sent me to help you,
knows you better than you know yourself.'

'And I'll be able to see the separation of the soul from
the body?'

'You shall see it. Your master will die soon, around ten
o'clock, or just after. They'll all believe that you've been
as far as Rennes and back (for you must say nothing of
our meeting), and they'll try to make you take some rest.
But refuse to go and lie down. Stay by the count's bedside
and don't take your eyes away from his face. When he dies,
you'll see his soul escape from his lips in the form of a
white mouse. This mouse will disappear straight away in
some hole. Don't worry about that. Go yourself to town to
fetch the funeral cross from the church, and don't let
anyone else go instead. When you're at the porch, wait
for the mouse to arrive. Don't go in the church before it.
Be content to follow it all the time. This is important. If

41

you strictly follow my advice, before nightfall you'll have learnt what you so wished to know. And now, Ludo Garel, goodbye!'

With that, the strange person disappeared into a faint mist which was soon confounded with the mist rising from the humid ground of the new-born day.

Ludo Garel went back to Quinquiz.

'God be praised,' said the master on seeing his servant. 'You've done right to be quick, my good man. I'm at the lowest ebb. If you'd been an hour later, you'd only have found a corpse. How did things go in Rennes?'

'You've won your lawsuit.'

'I thank you for your efforts, my friend. Thanks to you, I can die in peace.'

This time, Ludo Garel did not try to comfort his master with words of hope. He knew that his destiny must be accomplished. Sadly, he went and sat by the bedside where he would never lose sight of the count's face. The room was full of people in tears. The countess took Ludo by the arm and whispered in his ear:

'You're tired out. There's plenty of people here to watch over my poor husband. Go and sleep.'

'My duty is to stay at my master's bedside until his last breath,' replied the servant.

And he stayed there, despite their insistence.

The clock struck ten. Just as the young man had predicted, the Lord of Quinquiz began his death struggle. An old woman intoned the prayers; the others murmured the responses. Ludo Garel mixed his voice with the others', but his mind was not on the prayer; it was tensely awaiting what was about to happen, when the soul would leave the body.

The count, however, began to turn his head to left and right. This was because he could hear death coming, without knowing from which direction.

Suddenly he stiffened; death had touched him.

He let out a long sigh, and Ludo saw his soul exhaled from between his lips in the form of a white mouse.

The man from the cemetery had told the truth.

The mouse, moreover, just appeared and then disappeared.

The old woman who had intoned the prayers, took up the *De profundis.* Ludo took advantage of the emotion caused by the count's final end, to slip away, and to run along a footpath which was a short-cut to the town. At Quinquiz, they had still not told anyone to go and fetch the funeral cross, by the time he reached the church. The white mouse arrived, and he let it go inside first. It ran quickly, but he was able to follow it without too much trouble. Three times he followed it right round the church. At the end of the third tour, it went out by the porch. Ludo hurried after it, with the funeral cross, which he had taken on passing, held against his chest. The little bells on the cross went tinkle, tinkle, and the mouse went scamper, scamper. The mouse, the cross, and Ludo who was carrying it, ran together across the fields to Quinquiz. The little white mouse jumped over each gate, just as the master did when he was alive; then it ran right round the edge of each field.

As soon as the tour of the fields was accomplished, it set off towards the manor. First of all, it went into an isolated building where the farming implements were kept*. It put its paws on all of them; ploughs, mattocks, spades, it said goodbye to them all.

Then it went into the house.

Ludo saw it climb up on to the corpse and let itself be put in the coffin with it.

The clergy came for the body. The funeral mass was sung; the coffin was lowered into the grave. But just as the priest had sprinkled it with holy water, and the close relatives had thrown the first handfuls of earth, Ludo saw the white mouse come out.

The unknown young man had expressly told him to follow it to the end, even through brambles, thorns and mire.

He had to leave the burial and set out again on pilgrimage after the mouse.

They crossed woods, went over mires, jumped over ditches, went through towns, until at last they came to a great heath in the middle of which was a half-dead tree trunk. It was so old, so bare, that one couldn't be sure if it were the trunk of a beech or a chestnut. It was hollow. Truly, it only stood up by a miracle. What was left of its bark was cracked from top to bottom. The mouse slipped in through one of these cracks, and there and then Ludo saw the Lord of Quinquiz appear in the hollow trunk.

'My poor master!' he exclaimed, wringing his hands. 'What

---

*The Master of Quinquiz was apparently one of those gentlemen farmers, quite numerous in Lower Brittany, who would go to the fields with their sword by their side, hang it on a tree, and set to work with the plough just like their farm labourers.

The departure of the soul.

are you doing there?'

'My dear Ludo, every man must do his penitance in the place God assigns him to.'

'Is there any way at all that I can help you?'

'Yes, there is.'

'What?'

'Fast for me for a year and a day. If you do that, I shall be delivered for always, and your beatitude will follow close on mine.'

'I'll do it,' replied Ludo Garel.

He kept his promise and he died as soon as his fast was accomplished."

(Told by Marie-Louise Bellec, seamstress, Port-Blanc.)

- § -

Chapter 7. After death.

Not long ago, when someone died, their body was laid out on the kitchen table, near the window. A white sheet was placed under the body and two others were hung from the ceiling beams on either side of the table, and they pinned sprigs of mistletoe or laurel here and there.

- § -

At the time when they still used to lay out the dead on the kitchen table, they placed the head on a pillow of oat chaff. The body was always covered by one of the large cloths that were normally used to cover the bread to keep the sun off it, and protect it from dust.

These cloths were generally of a fairly fine material and decorated with a red or blue cross woven in the fabric.

- § -

For the funeral attire of the dead, they began by putting a white shirt on the corpse. On old men they would add a nightcap. If it were a woman, they would first comb and smooth out the hair, and then put on her best hat, as well as her collaret and her blouse front.

As for the shrouding itself, it consisted in wrapping the lower half of the body in a clean sheet, almost as one would a child, in such as way that the arms stayed free and the legs were not too fettered.

Then they placed the palms of the hands together, and wrapped a string of beads - their own if possible - around the wrists.

- § -

The people who do the shrouding are almost always the same in each locality. It's a sort of sacramental function. They say they are warned by a mysterious intuition that their services are going to be needed in such and such a place, before the messenger who is being sent for them has finished tying his shoe laces.

Old Lena Bitoux, from Kermaria, would be half way there when they sent someone for her. When she met them, she would say:

'Yes, yes, I know all about it; don't waste your breath.'

- § -

After death.

The story of the verger from Névez.

"In the old days, in the small villages, it was always the verger who put the dead in the coffin.

One day when the verger of Névez was on his way back to church, where he was going to arrange a burial after having put a corpse in its coffin, he saw a man sitting on a roadside gate, dressed in his Sunday clothes, his head hanging low.

'Good day, Jean-Louis,' said the man, lifting his head.

'What!' cried the stupified verger, 'it's you, Joachim!'

It was the same dead man whom he had put in the coffin a few minutes before, after having dressed him in his best clothes.

'Yes, it's really me,' replied Joachim. 'I came here to look out for you, and tell you that you must do your task again.'

'You're not all right, the way I put you?'

'No, you bent my left arm behind my back; I can't go away in that posture.'

Having said that, he disappeared. The verger went back to the house, and, to the great scandal of the family, re-opened the coffin. What Joachim had said was true: the left arm was bent behind the body. The verger put everything in order and set out again towards the town. When he passed by the gate, he saw that the dead man was still there, but this time he was standing with his head held high.

'Perhaps I've missed something else?' the verger asked himself.

But no; the dead man simply waved his hand as a sign that he was taking his leave.

'God give you happiness!' said the verger, lifting his hat.

And that's all."

(Told by Coudray, Coray).

- § -

46

After death.

The vicar's wake.

"I always remember this date; it was the twentieth of February. I was taking part in the vicar's wake. He was a worthy man, and he had died that very morning. With me there was Fanch the carpenter, and Marie-Cinthe, an old flax spinner.

The dead man was sitting in an armchair, dressed in his best attire. He had a peaceful face, almost smiling.

We said the prayers individually, and softly.

The silence and lack of movement began to make me feel sleepy. Afraid that I would, in fact, fall asleep, I proposed to the others that we should recite the prayers together, so that we should keep one another awake.

The carpenter was pleased, but the old spinner, who was always contrary, preferred to move away from us, near to the hearth, where she continued alone.

Fanch and I stayed close to the corpse.

I started the prayers; he gave the responses.

Suddenly he motioned with his hand as if to tell me to be quiet and listen.

I leant my ear.

'Can't you hear it?' he asked me.

I could hear a little clear noise, silvery, but so faint, so faint... It could have been the ringing of far-off bells, of little bells with tones pure as crystal, ringing in the country, leagues away from us.

It lasted several seconds.

Then there was sweet music which seemed to come from the walls, the floor, the furnishings, from everywhere in the room.

Neither Fanch nor I had ever heard music so sweet.

Fanch looked to left and right, trying to see where it came from. But he saw nothing.

When the music ceased, I took up the prayers again; then we heard a new noise.

This time it was a long monotonous drone. We could have sworn that a swarm of bees had invaded the room and were going from one wall to the other to find a spot to settle.

'It's not possible,' said Fanch. 'There must be some bees in here.'

He took one of the candles which were burning in front of the corpse, lifted it above his head, and moved about the room, but although we looked in every corner, there was

47

After death.

not even the shadow of a fly.

The droning continued, sometimes strong and clear, sometimes faint, confused, and scarcely perceptible.

Fanch and I sat down again. We spent a long time just looking at one another, deep in thought.

We were not afraid, but we were troubled by the strangeness of these events. It was as though we were in a dream.

Suddenly, Marie-Cinthe's coarse voice startled us:

'You can come over here to warm yourselves, if you wish. I'll take your place next to the corpse.'

We asked her if she hadn't heard anything.

She replied in the negative.

And from that moment, we ourselves heard nothing more."

(Told by A.-M. L'Horset, Penvénan, 1889.)

- § -

Torfado's wake.

"During all his life, Lôn Torfado had done nothing but follow the precepts of Ollier Hamon (who was said to have been a good-for-nothing, a debauchee, and a braggart). Now Torfado was dead, and his wife tried in vain to persuade anyone from the neighbourhood to watch over his corpse.

'And yet I can't do it alone,' she said to herself; 'I'd be too afraid that he'd play a worse trick on me now that he's dead, than any he did when he was alive.'

It was already Saturday evening.

Although it was late in the day, Torfado's wife went to town. She thought:

'I'll find three or four bad characters at the inn; types like my husband was. They'll wish for nothing better than to play their part in his last night, as long as I offer them as much cider and brandy as they want.'

It happened just as she had predicted.

There was a group of noisy drinkers playing cards in the inn at the entrance to the town.

Torfado's wife crossed the threshold and said:

'Are there four charitable men amongst the Christians here, who will do something for me?'

'Yes,' replied one of the drinkers, 'as long as we don't have to sleep with you, for you're past it.'

'It's to keep watch over my husband who's just died. I'll give you as much cider and brandy as you like.'

48

After death.

'Well boys,' said the man to his friends, 'the innkeeper's threatened to throw us out on the stroke of nine. Let's follow this woman. We'll continue our party at her place, and the drink will cost us nothing.'

'Let's go!' cried the others.

Torfado's wife went back home, escorted by four half-drunk fellows who bawled their heads off all along the way.

'Here we are,' she said, opening the door. 'I beg you to be a little less noisy out of respect for the dead.'

He was there, the dead man, laid out on the kitchen table. They had thrown the bread cloth over him; it was the only suitable piece of cloth in the house. His face, however, was uncovered.

'Hey! But!' cried one of the improvised watchers. 'It's Lòn Torfado!'

'Yes,' replied the widow. 'He died this afternoon.'

She went to a cupboard, took out some bottles and glasses, set them out on the bench, and said:

'You can drink your fill. As for me, I'm off to bed.'

'Yes, yes, you can leave Torfado in our care. We'll make sure he doesn't escape.'

The woman left, and the men sat down at a little table placed near the corpse, on which a candle was burning and where there was a boxwood branch resting on a plateful of holy water.

I still haven't told you who they were. There was Fanch, Luch, and the Troadek brothers. They were all resolute and unafraid; types not to be affected by the presence of a corpse.

Fanch took a pack of cards from his jacket pocket; it went everywhere with him.

'Cut!' he said to one of the Troadeks.

And they started playing.

They played for an hour, drinking, cursing and swearing.

If at first they had only been half-drunk, they were quite drunk now, except for the youngest of the Troadeks, who had a little more decency than the others.

'All the same boys,' he said, 'what we're doing isn't good. Aren't you afraid we might regret the way we're behaving in front of a corpse? We haven't even said a prayer for his soul's rest.'

'Ha! ha! ha!' Luch laughed derisively; 'Torfado's soul! If he ever really had one, it would rather drink and play cards with us than listen to prayers!'

After death.

'Holy God, yes,' added Fanch. 'Torfado was a fine rogue, that he was. Dead as he is, I'm sure he'd still accept if we were to offer him a game of cards.'

'Don't say such things, Fanch.'

'We're going to see!'

Adding action to his words, he shuffled the cards and, as it was his turn to deal, he did so for five, instead of four.

'Old Torfado!' he exclaimed, 'there's a hand for you.'

Then something terrifying happened.

The dead man, whose hands were together on his chest, let his left arm slide little by little to the table, took his hand of cards and lifted them in front of his face, as if to look at them, then he played one, yelling at the same time in a formidable voice:

'Spades and trumps, I'll be damned! Spades and trumps! Spades and trumps!'

At first, our four jolly fellows were petrified with fright, but they soon found the door and, despite all his bragging, Fanch was not the last to leave. They threw themselves into the night without asking themselves which way they were going. They wandered about thus until dawn, like crazed bulls. When, with daylight, they each regained their homes, they all had their necks the colour of death. Fanch expired within a week. The others escaped death, but only after having suffered for almost a year from a mysterious fever which they could only cure by dint of taking the waters of Saint Gonery's spring."

(Told by Jean-Marie Corre, Penvénan, 1886.)

Chapter 8. Burial.

The empty house.

"A house should never be left empty during a funeral, or the dead person, whom one believes one is accompanying to the cemetery, may stay behind to guard it.

A butcher from Gouesnac'h owed one of the farmers of Clohars for a calf. One Saturday morning, he was passing close by, and said to himself:

'Well, I may as well make a detour and pay my debt to old Lharidon.'

Naic Lharidon was the name of the good woman who kept the farm with her two sons.

He took the road which went to her house. When he was in the yard, he was quite surprised to find no one about. 'Could they all be out on the land?' he asked himself. The door of the house was closed, which was unusual. He tried it; it opened, and he found himself in the kitchen, which seemed just as deserted as outside.

'Hello!' he cried; 'are you all dead here?'

'O dear, it's almost like that,' replied a hidden voice which he recognised as that of old Lharidon.

As it was very dark in the house, he asked:

'Where are you, Naic?'

'Here, in the corner by the hearth, butcher.'

He went closer and saw her stirring the cinders with the little iron fork they use in the country for putting branches of gorse on the fire.

'Well,' said the butcher, 'my business is only with you. I've brought you the money for your calf; do you want to count it? It's twenty-four francs, if I remember correctly.'

'Yes, yes, just leave it on the table.'

'As you wish... Good health to you, Naic, and till the next time; I'm in a hurry.'

'God grant that we meet again, butcher!'

Never had he found the old woman so accommodating. She had not even troubled to check the money, she who usually tried to get more than her due. Whilst making these reflections, the butcher approached the main road. Just as he reached it, he saw a group of mourners on their way back from Clohars. Amongst them were the old woman's two sons. He stopped to greet them as they passed.

'There's been a funeral today?' he asked them.

'Yes,' replied the eldest brother in a sad voice.

'One of your relatives, perhaps?... That must be why I

51

Burial.

found your mother stirring the cinders and looking so pre-occupied. She didn't even bother to count the money I'd brought her for the calf.'

The two brothers looked at him, stupefied.

'Did you say our mother?... You spoke of our mother?'

'Of course I did. What's so extraordinary about that, for you to stare at me so strangely?'

'But we've just buried her!'

It was the butcher's turn to stare.

'Yet I saw her just as clear as you are,' he affirmed.

Then the brothers' servant, who was also with them, said:

'Didn't I warn you that you shouldn't leave the house empty?... Now she won't go away until sunset.'

The brothers, and those who accompanied them, waited until sunset before going into the house. When they went in the kitchen, the dead one had left, but the butcher's money was there on the table, and the gorse fork was lying across the cinders on the hearthstone."

(Told by Joseph Mahé, Quimper.)

- § -

The hat.

"I can't tell you exactly how long ago this happened. My cousin Louis had arranged to supply several loads of straw to an innkeeper in Pontrieux. He had purchased this straw himself from Guern Manor. He arranged with the young men of the manor to make up the convoy, which consisted of four wagons. The road to Pontrieux is long, but there are plenty of inns, and the distances between them are short. Our straw conveyers didn't miss their pints; being young, they had good heads and thirsty throats. Once they had made the delivery at Pontrieux, they had a party; and if the wagons were empty on the way back, their wagoners were, on the other hand, somewhat full.

They sang and joked for as long as the day lasted. When night fell, they became quiet and walked silently alongside their bullocks. But you know how the worst drunkenness is the one which broods inside.

After eleven o'clock, when our people were crossing the town of Pommerit, my cousin Louis exclaimed:

'Well I'll be damned! The Pommerit girls have always had a reputation for dancing at night. Have they all gone to bed

52

with the chickens?'

'It's not true, boys,' said the eldest of the Guerns. 'There's one, two, three, four, five, six, seven, eight dancing there in the moonlight!'

He pointed his finger in the direction of the cemetery, which was by the roadside, and where black forms seemed to be undulating gracefully like Breton dancers.

'Hey!' said one of his brothers; 'they're only the crosses of tombs; they seem to move because you're staggering.'

'Perhaps they're the bunches of cypress that they put on noble's tombs,' said another.

'That's what we're going to find out!' yelled the eldest of the Guerns, as he lept up the cemetery steps in one bound.

A moment later, he came back clutching a white hat in his hand.

'Who was right?' he asked... 'But we've missed our opportunity; the pretty night-birds have flown away.'

Having said this, he stuffed the hat in his pocket.

All along the rest of the way they heard him repeating:

'Little hat of fine cloth, you must have graced a pretty face.... A pretty girl, no doubt... I only wish for one thing: that she'll come to Guern to claim it back.'

When the wagons were parked in the yard of the manor, and the bullocks attended to, the first thought of each of them was to go to bed. They were besotted with drink and tired out. The eldest son slept upstairs. He did not go to bed, however, until he had carefully folded the hat and put it in a corner of his cupboard.

When he woke up, his first thoughts were of the hat.

As he turned the key in the cupboard door, he took up his refrain of the night before:

'Little hat of fine cloth, you must have graced a...'

But the door was not fully open when he let out a cry... It was a cry of horror, of fear, enough to make the hair stand up on your head. Everyone in the house ran there. In place of the white hat of fine cloth, there was a skull. And it still had long and supple hair on it, showing it was that of a woman.

The eldest son was so pale that he looked green. Suddenly, he said with anger, whilst pretending to laugh:

'That's a nasty trick someone's played on me. To hell with this skull.'

He was already moving his hand forward to grab the skull and throw it outside, when its jaws moved and they heard a derisive voice:

'I've done what you asked, young man; I've come to Guern to claim back my hat. It's not my fault if you've changed your mind since last night.'

I promise you that the eldest son of the Guerns was no longer laughing, and that his anger had left him.

His mother, who was right behind him, pulled on his sleeve.

'Jozon,' she murmured, 'you've behaved like a rascal. Go at once, please, to the vicar. Only he can sort this out.'

The young man didn't need telling twice. He was only too anxious to get out of this difficult spot.

Half an hour later, he brought the vicar. The latter drew several crosses, muttered some latin words, then, taking the skull, he put it in the young man's hands.

'Go and put it back where it came from, in the charnel house of Pommerit. Set it down there on the stroke of midnight. You must take a child who has not yet been baptised with you. Gaud Keraudrenn was born last night, in the next hamlet. First go and ask them on my behalf, if they will entrust their new-born child to you. God give you grace to make amends!'

That very evening, Jozon Guern went back to Pommerit, with a skull in one hand, and a newly-born child under his other arm.

He was no longer singing: 'Little hat of fine cloth...'

He went quickly, and, as midnight struck, he put the skull back in the charnel house from which it had come.

Under his arm, the tiny little child cried, because of the cold, although he did his best to keep it covered with the side of his jacket.

'Ah,' cried the charnel house bones in chorus, 'you've had a clever idea bringing this child with you. If it wasn't that we've no right to deprive him of baptism, your bones and his would already be spread out amongst ours.'

Next day, the young man became godfather to the child. But when he returned home, he began to waste away. Death had looked on him from too close. He did not last a year.

(Told by Pierre Simon*, Penvénan, 1889).

---

*This story is true in its essentials; it's the story of a drunken boy who steals a skull from a charnel house and takes it home with him. The next morning he is horrified on finding it in his bedroom. He asks the vicar's advice. The latter tells him to do what is recounted above. It seems to have happened about 1860.

Chapter 9. The soul's lot.

To have sure information on the soul's lot after death, there is only:

1. The 'Agrippa.'
2. The 'ofern drantel' or 'thirtieth.'

The 'Agrippa.'

The 'Agrippa' is an enormous book. Stood on end, it is as tall as a man.

Its pages are red, its characters black. It must be signed by the devil in order to be effective.

It must be kept closed by a large padlock when it is not being consulted.

It is a dangerous book. It should not be kept free. They hang it by a chain from the strongest beam of its own room. The beam from which it hangs must not be straight; it must be bent or twisted.

The name of this book varies with the region. In Tréguier it is called the 'Agrippa;' around Chateaulin, the 'Egremont;' around Quimper, 'Ar Vif;' in Haute Léon, 'An Negromans;' and in Plouescat, the book of 'igromancerie.'

- § -

This book is alive. It does not like being consulted. One must be stronger than it, in order to extract its secrets.

One only sees the red until one has subdued it. The black characters only show themselves when one has constrained them to do so, by thrashing the book like a stubborn horse. One has to fight with it, and sometimes the struggle lasts for whole hours. One ends up covered in sweat.

- § -

He who has an 'Agrippa' cannot rid himself of it without a priest's help, and only at the time of death.

- § -

At first, only priests had 'Agrippas.' They each had their own. On waking up on the morning after their ordination, they found it on their bedside table, without their knowing how, or from where it had come.

Many ecclesiastics emigrated during the Revolution, and

55

some of their 'Agrippas' fell into the hands of ordinary literates who had learnt the art of using it. The latter pass them on to their descendants. This explains the presence of a 'strange book' in many farm houses.

The clergy know how many 'Agrippas' have gone astray, and they know the persons who keep them.

An old priest from Penvénan said:

'There are two 'Agrippas' in my parish which are not where they should be.'

The priest does nothing whilst the keeper is alive; but when death approaches, and he is called to his bedside, he speaks to him as follows:

'You will have a heavy burden to carry beyond the grave, unless you rid yourself of it in this world.'

Astonished, the dying man asks:

'What is this burden?'

'It's the burden of the 'Agrippa' you have in your house,' replies the priest. 'Give it up to me; if not, with such a load dragging behind you, you'll never get to paradise.'

It is rare for a dying man not to give up the 'Agrippa' straight away.

The 'Agrippa,' abandoned, seeks its own kind. It makes a great din all over the farm. But the priest exorcises it and makes it rest peacefully. Then he tells the people there to make a pile of straw. He lights it himself. The 'Agrippa' is soon reduced to ashes. The priest collects these ashes, seals them in a sachet, and places the latter around the dying man's neck, saying:

'May this be light for you!'

- § -

It is difficult for a vicar to sleep in peace whilst there remains even one 'Agrippa' in other hands.

- § -

You don't have to be a priest to know when someone who is not a priest has an 'Agrippa.'

The man who has an 'Agrippa' has a special smell. He smells of sulphur and smoke, because of his dealings with devils. That's why they keep away from him.

- § -

The soul's lot.

The 'Agrippa' which kept coming back.

"Loizo-goz, of Penvénan, had one which greatly embarrassed him; he couldn't wish for anything better than to pass it on to someone else. He offered it to a farmer from Plouguiel. The latter accepted the offer.

One night, they all heard a terrible din. It was Loizo-goz dragging his 'Agrippa' to Plouguiel by its chain.

Loizo-goz sang happily on his way back. He felt as though a weight had been lifted from his heart. But he had scarcely returned home when all his happiness left him; the 'Agrippa' had already come back and taken up its old place.

Some time later, Loizo-goz made a great fire of straw and threw the evil book in it. But instead of devouring the book, the flames drew away from it.

'Since fire won't do it, let's try water,' said Loizo-goz to himself.

He dragged the book to the beach, climbed into a boat, went out to sea, and threw his 'Agrippa' overboard, with several large stones tied to it to weight it down.

'There!' he thought; 'this time we'll be parted for ever.'

He was wrong.

As he was crossing the beach, he heard the sound of a chain dragging over the pebbles behind him. It was the book which had managed to rid itself of the large stones. He saw it whizz past him like an arrow. Back home, he found it hanging from its beam. The cover and the pages were all dry. It was as though the water had not even touched it.

He had to resign himself to keeping his 'Agrippa.'"

(Told by Baptiste Geffroy, Penvénan, 1886).

- § -

The 'Agrippa' contains the names of all the devils, and teaches how to conjure them up.

Thanks to it, one can know if a defunct soul is damned.

When a priest has just buried someone, he goes straight away to consult his 'Agrippa.' All the demons come running when their names are called. The priest questions them one after the other: 'Have you taken the soul of so-and-so?' If they all say 'no,' then the soul is saved. To send them away, the priest calls them again by their names, beginning with the name of the one who was last to come, and so on.

57

The soul's lot.

The 'ofern drantel,' or 'thirtieth'.

In the old days they used to celebrate thirty services for every person who died. The priests said the first twenty-nine masses in their parish church; but it was the custom to say the thirtieth in the Chapel of Saint Hervé on top of the Ménez-Bré (or high mountain). It is this thirtieth mass that the Bretons call 'Ann ofern drantel.'

It is celebrated at midnight. They say it backwards, starting with the end.

They only light a single candle on the altar.

All the dead of the year go to this mass; all the devils appear there also.

The priest who goes to say it must be both very learned and very brave. He takes his shoes off at the foot of the mountain, and climbs it barefooted, for he must be 'priest right to the ground.' He climbs with a silver basin of holy-water in one hand, and a sprinkler in the other, with which he makes continual aspersions. Often, he finds it hard to go forwards, so much do the dead souls press in on him, avid to receive a few drops of holy-water to give themselves a brief respite.

On the previous day, he has had a bag of linseed taken to the chapel.

Once the mass has been said, he starts calling the devils from the porch. They come running, yelling wildly. It is a terrible moment. Woe to him if he loses his head! He makes the demons be silent, lines them all up in single file, and obliges them to show their claws so that he can see if the soul of the defunct for whom he has celebrated the 'ofern drantel' is in their possession. Then he sends them away one at a time, giving each one a grain of linseed, for devils will never agree to go away with their hands empty. If he makes a single omission he is obliged, in exchange, to give himself up, incurring his own damnation.

- § -

Imprudence.

"One evening, a young priest who was still a newcomer to these matters, imprudently gave himself the task of going to the 'Ménez-Bré' to say the 'ofern-drantel.'

Unfortunately, he became confused.

The soul's lot.

Straight away, the devils hurled themselves on him.

By a providential chance, Tadik-Coz was still praying in his vicarage at Bégard, some two leagues from Bré. Having heard a noise coming from the direction of the mountain, he listened carefully:

'Ha, ha!' he said to himself; 'there's a fight going on up there!'

He quickly saddled his Cornish cob, which went like the wind.

When he reached the chapel, the devils were already dragging the young priest through a breech they had made in the gable.

However, Tadik-Coz was able to grab hold of one of his poor brother's legs. The devils did not try to fight him. They had learnt only too well to fear him. The sight of him alone set them to flight. They disappeared with cries of rage. The young priest was saved. Tadik-Coz was content to give him a quiet telling off:

'My child,' he said to him, 'you should wait until you have our experience, before doing the things we, the old ones do. Let this be a lesson to you!'"

(Told on the 'Ménez-Bré' by R. Auffret, 1889.)

- § -

Tadic-Coz.

"This Tadik-Coz was a master of the 'ofern drantel.' They say that since his death, there have been no more priests who know how to say it.

Once, when he had just said the 'thirtieth' mass for the soul of a dead villager, he saw, whilst reviewing the demons, that one of them was clutching the soul of this particular person. Anyone else but Tadik-Coz would have said:

'The soul is damned; nothing more can be done about it.' But Tadik-Coz was not a man to be put off easily. I really believe that, to save a soul, he would have gone barefooted into hell.

'Hey, friend,' he said to the demon, 'you look quite proud of what you're holding there. Quite frankly, I don't see why you're so proud. I knew the defunct when he was still in this world. In truth, he was a poor wretch! He's already had such misery during his life, that your hell will seem to him more like a place of delights. When one has suffered as he has on earth, one hasn't much to fear, not even from an eternity of torments.'

'That's somewhat true,' replied the demon. 'I don't take any pleasure in annoying him. To tell the truth, I could think of nothing better than to make a swop.'

'I'll make a swop with you.'

'Whose soul will you swop for his?'

'Mine..., but on one condition!'

'Go on.'

'This is it. You devils think you're very clever. Rightly or wrongly, I also consider that I'm not an imbecile. Let's bet that you can't catch me out!'

'Agreed.'

'Let's be quite clear about it. If I lose, my soul is yours; if I win, I keep it. In either case, the one you're holding there no longer belongs to you, so you can start by letting it go.'

The devil let go of the soul, which flew off lightly, asking a thousand blessings for Tadik-Coz.

'Let's start,' said the latter, 'I'm waiting!'

The devil scratched his ear.

'Well,' he said at last, 'show me something I've never seen before.'

'That's all! At least you're not hard to please.'

Tadik-Coz put his hand in his pocket, and pulled out an apple and a knife. He cut the apple in two. Then, showing the inside of the fruit to the devil, who was taken aback, he said:

'See that!'

And, as the devil did not seem to understand, he added:

'No doubt you've seen the inside of plenty of apples, but you've certainly not seen inside this one before!'

The demon was crestfallen; he had to admit he had lost, and Tadik-Coz went back to his vicarage rubbing his hands with glee."

(Told by Naïc Fulup, 1889.)

- § -

When Tadic-Coz celebrated the 'thirtieth' on the 'Ménez-Bré,' the entire mountain lighted up so that it was clear as daylight.

- § -

Chapter 10. The drowned.

The drowned whose bodies have not been recovered and buried in consecrated ground, wander eternally all along the coasts.

It is not unusual to hear them crying pitifully in the night: 'Iou!Iou!'

Then the people say:

'E-man Iannic-ann-ôd o iouall' (it's Iannic-ann-ôd - Little John of the Beach - who's howling).

All these drowned howlers are called Iannic-ann-ôd, without distinction.

Iannic-ann-ôd is not evil, provided one does not amuse oneself by sending his plaintive call back to him. Woe to the imprudent who risk this game. If you reply once, Iannic-ann-ôd leaps half the distance separating him from you, in a single bound; if you reply a second time, he leaps half of the remaining distance; if you reply a third time, he breaks your neck.

- § -

Iannic-ann-ôd.

"One summer evening, a farm worker was on his way back after taking the cattle to the fields, for it was the time when the latter stayed out all night. As he was walking along a footpath by the beach, he heard the footsteps of Iannic-ann-ôd on the pebbles. The farm worker was a jolly, stout-hearted fellow. He knew all the stories they told in the long winter evenings about Iannic-ann-ôd, and he had promised himself he would put them to the test at the first opportunity.

'Now,' he said to himself, 'I'll clear this up for myself.'

As he knew of the danger, he waited until he was close enough to the farm, before answering the shrill 'Iou' coming from the beach prowler behind him.

Only then did he let out a sonorous 'Iou' in his turn.

No doubt Iannic-ann-ôd was not used to such audacity, for he shut up suddenly. The farm worker noticed, in return, that he was much closer. His silhouette appeared at the other end of the footpath, all black in the moonlight.

He started howling again, louder than ever.

This time, the farm worker only answered the call when he had reached the middle of the farm yard.

Iannic-ann-ôd appeared at the gate.

61

The drowned.

He yelled with increasing rage:
'Iou! Iou! Iou!'
There was provocation in his cry.
The farm worker started running fast, as fast as if he had wings on his heels.
When he reached the threshold of the house, he let out the third 'Iou,' whilst closing the door with the heavy oak bar.
A formidable blow fell on the outside of the door; one would have sworn it was going to break in pieces. And the howler's voice rose menacingly:
'You've got away this time; but if you ever come back, I'll have you!'
The farm worker took him at his word."
(Told by René Alain, Quimper, 1889)

Jean Duigou's luck.

"Jean Duigou the fisherman was fishing one night in the Brest roads, some cable lengths from the shore, all alone in his boat. Suddenly, a prolonged howl came from one of the woods by the shore. He thought it was some joker who was trying to scare him, and he replied with a similar howl.
The same cry came a second time; he answered it again.
'He's beginning to irritate me, this scurvy monkey,' he said to himself. 'If he does it again, I'll counter it with a "coc'h" that will be heard far and wide.'
He had not finished talking to himself like that, when the invisible person howled a third time:
'Iou...ou...ou!'
Then Jean Duigou, bellowed with all his might:
'Coc'h evid-ou...ou...out' (Shit to you!)
But the last word stuck in his throat. Someone was in the boat behind him, with his hands around his neck in a grip of steel. The fisherman's face became covered in sweat.
'Whoever you are, in the name of God, let go!' he begged.
'Yes, I'll let you go, but only because you invoked the name of God... If your boat hadn't been made of oak, you'd have been done for,' said the other.
Having said this, he relaxed his fingers and disappeared.
Jean Duigou was lucky. He saw that what the old folks say is true; oak wood is a precious talisman against evil spirits."
(Told by Pierre Le Goff, Argol.)

Chapter 11. The violently-killed and the hanged.

Whenever an accident followed by immediate death occurs on a road, a cross should be erected by the spot; if not, the soul of the dead person will only be appeased by a similar accident at the same place. That is why there are so many stone, and wooden crosses on the roadsides in Brittany.

In Cornouaille it is the custom to throw a stone on the bank in front of these 'crosses of misfortune.'

- § -

Any instrument whatever, which has been used to commit a murder, will invariably wound anyone who tries to use it later for its normal purpose.

- § -

The death stick.

"A pig dealer who had lost his walking-stick, was given one as a present by another dealer. Now that same evening, as he was walking to his inn for supper, the stick he had been given caught between his legs causing him to fall and hit his head on the pavement, where he lay half-dead. It was four or five weeks before he recovered.

But he had scarcely started to make the rounds of the markets when his new stick began to play tricks on him again. In the end, he said it was not natural, and decided not to use this evil stick any more. He hung it near the hearth by its leather wrist-strap.

Time went by, months, perhaps years. One winter's day when it was freezing hard, our man was visited by a farmer who had come on business. There was a bottle of cider open, and, as the visitor was paralysed with cold, our man invited him to sit by the fire with him, and have a drink.

Suddenly, just as the farmer was sitting down in the corner by the hearth, the stick fell by itself at the man's feet.

'What's this?' he said as he picked it up and examined it. 'If you don't mind my asking, where did you get this?'

'One of the other dealers gave it to me not long ago, and I can't say that it was a good present,' said the pig dealer.

'Why not?'

'Because that accursed piece of holly has given me nothing but trouble.'

And he told him all about it. When he had finished, the

farmer asked him:

'Would you tell me the name of the dealer who gave it to you?'

'You must know him; he lives near you. He's called Jacques Bourdoullouz. Does that interest you, then?'

'Very much, and you'll understand why... But first of all, I don't think you've forgotten that my father was found dead on the beach at Saint Efflam, with his skull smashed in.'

'Of course I haven't; they made a lot of noise about it at the time. If I remember rightly, they never did find out who killed him.'

'Nor the murder weapon, either. The medical expert said it could only have been a heavy hammer or one of these walking sticks with a heavy iron head. Now my father was never without his stick, but it wasn't found by his body; the murderer must have taken it with him after committing the crime. That stick was marked with two crossed notches on the head... Well, look at this!'

The farmer passed it to the dealer; the two notches forming a cross were still there, worn, but visible.

'This must be the one,' he murmured. 'I'm not surprised. What are you going to do?'

'Will you lend it to me?'

'You can take it and keep it; I don't want to see it again.'

They forgot about their business. The farmer went straight to the gendarmes. That same evening, Bourdoullouz was unexpectedly confronted with the accusing instrument. He was constrained to confess his crime, and they hanged him. God have mercy on him."

(Told by Fanchon ar Fulup, Ploumillau, 1893.)

- § -

The hanged one.

"There were two young men. One was called Cado, the other, Philip. They were both from the same parish, and they had done everything together since childhood. Having been everywhere together, they had become the best friends in the world. Whenever one of them appeared, the young girls would laugh and say:

'The other can't be far away.'

One would have had to go a long way to find a friendship more perfect than theirs.

64

The violently-killed and the hanged.

They had sworn that the first of them to be married would take the other as his best man.

'I'll be damned, if I don't keep my word,' they had said to each other.

The time came when they fell in love, and they had the misfortune to do so with the same heiress. Their friendship did not suffer at all from this. They each courted beautiful Marguerite Omnès, without running one another down; often keeping company with her old mother, and drinking one an-others health with the bowlfuls of cider Marguerite poured for them.

'Choose which one of us you like most, and you'll make one of us happy without making the other jealous,' they would say.

Despite all these fine assurances, Marguerite was most em-barrassed.

However, she had to make up her mind.

One day when Cado went there alone, she made him sit at the kitchen table, and, sitting herself opposite him, she said:

'Cado, I look on you as a good friend, and have a high opinion of you. You'll always be welcome in my house; don't let this upset you, but we'll never be husband and wife.'

'Ah!' he replied somewhat taken aback, 'then you've chosen Philip...'

He tried not to look upset, and to control his feelings, but the blow was unexpected, and it struck him right in the heart.

After a few banal words, he left, staggering like a drunken man, although his lips had scarcely touched the glass that Marguerite had filled for him. When he had left the Omnès' yard and was alone on the narrow path which led to his home, he began weeping like a child. He said to himself, 'what's the use of living, now?' And he resolved to die. All the same, he first wanted to shake hands with Philip and be the first to tell him of his good fortune.

Instead of going home, he took another footpath which led to Philip's house. His mother was peeling potatoes for the evening meal. She was astonished on seeing Cado looking so pale and unhappy:

'What's wrong with you?' she asked, 'you're as white as a sheet.'

'That's because you're seeing me in the evening mist. I've come to ask what Philip's thinking of doing tomorrow.'

'I honestly can't tell you. Right now he's taking a newly-born baby to be baptised!'

'I don't believe it.'

'Yes. It's the Nanes girl; she's had another bastard. They had to knock on three doors before they could find a god-father. It was Philip who accepted. I thought he should have refused to do it, like the others, but he didn't want to listen to my advice. I pointed out to him that evil tongues might say he was the child's father, but he got dressed and went off to town. When he was leaving, he swore he would ring the bells' (which was not done for illegitimate children).

The old woman had not finished speaking when they heard the bells ringing in the distance.

'What did I just say!...' exclaimed the old woman, when she heard them.

She went on:

'My son's hare-brained. You should take him in hand, Cado. You're more serious than him. I often worry that his heed-less ways will get him into trouble.'

'Don't worry,' replied Cado, 'I can assure you, on the con-trary, that he must have been born under a lucky star.'

And, wishing her good evening, he turned to go; he stop-ped on the threshold for a moment, and said:

'Please ask Philip to meet me at dawn tomorrow, where the paths cross on the High Moor.'

The High Moor is a hillock with gorse and poor grass, where the poor people graze their cattle. Two paths cross one another at the foot of a cross. It was to this cross that Cado went, after having been home for a halter, saying it was for bringing the grey mare back from the fields. He tied the halter to one of the arms of the cross, and hanged himself.

When, at dawn on the next day, Philip went to the meet-ing place, it was to find his friend's body swinging between heaven and earth.

At that time it was strictly forbidden to touch a man who had voluntarily killed himself.

Philip went back to tell them of the terrible thing that had happened. When he told the Omnès, Marguerite wept bitter tears.

'Ah!' exclaimed the young man, 'he's the one you loved!'

'You're wrong, friend,' replied Marguerite's mother who was smoking her pipe by the hearth. 'Marguerite told Cado yesterday afternoon that, whatever friendship she felt for

The violently-killed and the hanged.

him, it was you that she would marry.'

This was a great balm to Philip's heart.

The wedding-day was fixed there and then, but because of Cado's sad death, it was agreed there would be no dancing, and they would simply have a meal at the inn.

A week later, Philip set out in the company of another young man on a 'tour of invitations.' They were passing by the High Moor in the evening, when Philip suddenly put his hands to his forehead.

'I swore to Cado that he, and no one else, would be best man at my wedding. I must invite him. It's a useless formality, I know; but at least I'll have kept my word. It will help my salvation in the next world.'

And he began to climb the slope.

The corpse was already quite damaged, but it was still swinging at the end of the rope. Clouds of crows flew off as Philip approached.

'Cado,' he said, 'I'm getting married on Wednesday morning. I swore to have you as best man. I've come to invite you, so that you'll know I've kept my word. There'll be a place for you at the Rising Sun Inn.'

Having said that, Philip went back to his companion who was waiting at some distance, and the crows came back to eat Cado's remains in peace. Philip would willingly have invited his new godchild, but the poor little one had already died.

The wedding-day arrived. In his happiness, the new husband only had eyes for his young wife, who was surely the prettiest girl one could find. For certain, Philip was no longer thinking of Cado, and hadn't he put his mind to rest about that? The wedding feast was going well; the food was good, and the cider looked like gold in the glasses. The guests began to chat noisily. They had drunk the couple's health, and Philip was about to reply to the guests, when all of a sudden he saw a skeleton's arm raised before him, whilst a sinister mocking voice said:

'To my best friend!'

Horror of horrors! Cado's ghost was sitting in the place that had been reserved for him.

The husband went pale. His glass fell from his hands and broke into a thousand pieces.

His wife Marguerite; she also went whiter than a sheet.

A painful silence filled the room.

The innkeeper, surprised to see them no longer eating or

67

drinking, said in a disgruntled voice:

'But help yourselves; it's all for you, and what you don't have will still have to be paid for.'

No one answered him.

Cado stood up alone, and addressed himself to Philip:

'Why am I not welcome here? Didn't you invite me? Am I not your best man?'

And as Philip remained silent, looking down at his plate, he went on:

'I've nothing to say to the others here, and I don't want to spoil their pleasure any longer. I'm going. But you, Philip; I've the right to ask you why. I want you to meet me again on the High Moor, at midnight tonight. Be on time. If you don't turn up, I'll come after you.'

A second later, and the skeleton had disappeared.

The guests were relieved by its disappearance, but all the same, the weddiing ended on a sad note. The guests left as quickly as possible, and Philip was left there alone with his young wife. They were not rejoicing; he was, as they say, down in the mouth.

'Marguerite,' he said, 'you've heard Cado's ghost. What do you think I should do?'

She lowered her head and pondered, and then replied:

'It will be an unpleasant experience, but it would be best to know what it's all about right away. Go there, Philip, and may God go with you.'

The husband gave his new wife a long embrace, and, as it was already late, he set out in the clear of the night. The moon was white. Philip walked heart-broken, filled with a sinister foreboding. He thought: 'This is the last time I'll ever walk this path. Before long, Marguerite will marry again, a widow and a virgin.' He gave himself up to painful thoughts of this kind until, just at the foot of the High Moor, he found himself face to face with a white knight.

'Good evening, Philip,' said the knight.

'And the same to you,' replied the young man, 'although I don't seem to know you as well as you know me.'

'Don't be surprised that I know your name. I could also tell you where you're going.'

'It seems you know everything better than I do; for I don't really know where I'm going.'

'At least you're going to the meeting Cado arranged with you. Climb up behind me; my horse is strong enough to take a double load, and two's company is better than one.'

The violently-killed and the hanged.

All this seemed quite strange to Philip. But he was so lost! And then, the knight spoke with such a tender voice! He let himself be persuaded, jumped on the horse, and held on by clasping his arms around the unknown one's body. They were at the top of the hill in the winking of an eye. The gallows stood out before them in black against a silver sky, and the hanging body, which was nothing more than a skeleton, was swinging in the night breeze.

'Now get down,' said the white knight to Philip. 'Go to Cado's skeleton without fear, and touch its right foot with your right hand saying: "Cado, you called me; I've come; speak if you wish; what do you want of me?"'

Philip did and spoke as he had just been told.

Straight away, Cado's skeleton began kicking about with a noise of rattling bones, and a sepulchral voice yelled:

'A curse on him who taught you. If you hadn't met him on your way here, I'd be on the way to Heaven now, and you would have taken my place here on this gibbet!'

Philip went back to the knight, safe and well, and told him of Cado's curse.

'That's all right,' replied the white knight. 'Climb on my horse again.'

They went down the slope at a gallop.

'This is where I met you,' said the unknown one, 'and this is where I leave you. Go back to your wife. Live with her in wisdom, and never refuse to help poor people who seek your aid. I'm the child you took to be baptised. You can see how God can make an angel from a bastard. You did me a great service by consenting to be my godfather when others had refused. I've just returned you an equal favour. We're quits. Till we meet again.....'"

(Told by Lise Bellec, Port-Blanc.)

Chapter 12. The 'Anaon.'

The enormous population of souls in pain is called the 'Anaon.' (Note: This word is, strictly speaking, plural, referring to 'souls;' it is often treated as a singular word, in which case it refers to souls as a collectivity.)

- § -

The 'Anaon' is referred to, in association with every act of Breton life, including even the end of the wedding feast.

- § -

It's not good to sweep the house after sunset. There is a risk of sweeping out, with the dust, the souls of the dead which have often been able to enter their old homes at that time of the day.

- § -

It is good to leave a little fire burning in the ashes, in case a dead soul wishes to warm itself up in front of the hearth of it's former home.

- § -

As long as it's daylight, the earth is for the living; after dark it belongs to the souls of the dead. Honest people go to sleep with all their doors closed at the ghostly hour. One should never stay unnecessarily outdoors after sunset. The most untimely hours are between ten at night and two in the morning.

- § -

When one is about to go over a bank planted with gorse, one should take care to make a noise, to cough for example, to warn the souls which are perhaps doing penitence there, and to give them a chance to move aside. Before starting to cut a field of corn, one should say: 'If the 'Anaon' is here, peace be with it!'

- § -

The souls who do their penitence on earth are as close-pressed as the leaves of grass in a field or the drops of water in a shower.

- § -

The 'Anaon.'

The two friends.

"Two farm workers from Botsorhel, Pierre and Francois, had such a great friendship for each other that they had nothing to hide from one another and shared everything they had, hardships as well as pleasures. They had been living like that for ten years, in the most perfect unity, without ever having had the slightest argument.

'Only death can separate us,' they would say.

They had sworn to each other that, God willing, the first of them to die would come back to tell the other of his lot in the other world.

It was Pierre whom the 'Ankou' struck first. He was taken with a malignant fever when he was scarcely twenty-five years old. Throughout his illness, Francois never left his bed-side; he didn't leave his grave until the grave digger had finished levelling off the ground.

The night after the burial, he went to bed at his usual time, but did not sleep. He was too busy thinking where his friend might be, what he might be doing, and if he was not too sad to be parted from the living. He was also prevented from going to sleep by the thought that he was waiting for a visit from Pierre, and not for anything in the world would he wish him to find him asleep.

As he was dwelling on these things, heart-broken, he heard footsteps on the yard paving. Straight away he knew that it was his friend coming back to him. Almost immediately, the door opened in the stable where he slept.

'I can't have been wrong,' he thought.

Anxious as he was to see the one he loved again, he still felt a shiver come over him, when the voice that was dear to him asked in the darkness:

'Are you asleep, Francois?'

'No, Pierre, I'm not asleep. I've been lying awake waiting for you.'

'Well get up and come with me.'

Francois wasn't worried where he might be taking him, and he got up straight away. As soon as he was dressed, he went towards the door where he saw Pierre standing on the doorstep dressed in his shroud. Whilst he was looking at him in this sad attire, Pierre said to him:

'Yes, my friend, from now on this shroud is all I possess, alas.'

'And how do you find your new place?'

71

'That's why I've come for you, for I can let you see for yourself, if you'll agree to it, but I'm not allowed to tell you about it.'

'I'm ready. Let's go,' said Francois.

His friend took him quickly to the mill-pond at Goazwad, which was about a quarter of an hour from the farm. When they reached the water's edge, the ghost said to his friend:

'Take all your clothes off, including your boots.'

'What for?' asked the other, a little worried.

'To go in the water with me.'

'Whatever are you thinking of? It's quite a cold night; the water's deep, and I can't swim.'

'Don't worry, you won't have to swim.'

'All right; whatever happens, I've resolved to follow you wherever you go.'

At that same moment, the ghost jumped in the pond, and the living one went with him. They both sank and sank until their feet touched the bottom. Pierre held Francois by the hand. The latter was quite astonished to breathe under the water as easily as in the air. But he was shivering all over, and his teeth were chattering like pebbles thrown together. It was bitterly cold in that icy pond.

After they had been there about an hour, Francois, was feeling paralysed, and he said:

'Do I have to stay here long?'

'Are you in so much of a hurry to leave me?' replied the other.

'No; and you know very well that I'm never happier than when we're together... But it's bitterly cold and I'm suffering more than I can tell.'

'Well then, triple your suffering, and you'll have a faint idea of what mine's like.'

'Poor Pierre!'

'And I can tell you that you're reducing mine by your presence, and that you're shortening my time here by sharing it.'

'Then I'll stay for as long as it takes.'

'You'll be free to go when you hear the bells in the morning.'

At last the bells rang. Francois found himself safe and sound at the spot where he had left his clothes.

'Goodbye!' said his friend, whose head alone came out of the water. 'You can see me tonight, if you feel courageous enough to do the same thing again.'

'I'll wait for you like I did last night,' replied Francois.

And he went to work in the fields with the other farm workers, just as though he had spent the night in bed. When night came, he went to bed fully dressed, so as to be ready as soon as his friend called him. The latter appeared at the same time as on the night before, and the two of them went to the mill-pond. Once there, everything happened as on the previous night, except that the suffering of the living one was twice as cruel as before.

'Will your courage last out for one more time? Just once more?' the ghost asked him.

'I'll be faithful right to the end, even if it kills me,' said Francois.

When he went to start work, the master of the farm was struck by his pale and worn-out appearance.

'He must be spending his nights by his friend's grave at the cemetery,' he thought.

And he promised himself he would watch him that same evening. He had to wait till midnight. Then he saw the ghost cross the yard in the moonlight, push the stable door open, go inside, and come out with Francois. He followed the two as they went towards the mill. A clump of willows, which overhung the pond, permitted him to watch them jump in, and to listen to their underwater conversation:

'I can't go on any longer! I can't take any more!' groaned Francois.

And the other never stopped repeating to his friend:

'Be brave! Be brave!'

'No! I'm weakening. I'll never last till morning.'

'Yes, yes! Be strong! Only two hours more... Only an hour and a half.., and thanks to you I'll be delivered! Just think of that. Your troubles will be over; you'll have opened the way for me, and you'll not be long in joining me.'

The farmer was sweating behind his willow; a sweat of agony. He wanted to run away, but he didn't dare move. At last, the sky whitened and the bells of Botsorhel rang. Immediately, two loud cries came from the bottom of the mill-pond: 'Francois!...' 'Pierre!...'

And the farmer saw a kind of smoke come out of the water and rise up and lose itself in the clouds. Francois, on the other hand, fell exhausted, almost at his feet. He jumped to his aid, helped him to dress and, as he could not walk, carried him to the farm, where he had just time to receive the last rites before breathing his last breath."

(Told by Jean Dénès, Guerlesquin.)

73

The enchanted hare.

"All ruined castles have their enchanted hare.

These hares are the souls of former lords who are doing their penitence under this form. They have been condemned to become the most timid of animals after their death, because they terrorised everyone during their lives. They are only delivered when they have had as much pain inflicted on them by hunters, who shoot at them without knowing what they are, as they inflicted on other poor people who were formerly in their domain.

The lead-shot passes through them without killing them, and without causing loss of blood; but each time they suffer just as much as if they had been killed.

One day, when Jerome Lhostis of Pluzunet was hunting at Coatnizan, he started an outsize hare which ran off and sought refuge in the dovecote.

'Good!' he thought happily, 'it's as good as in my bag.'

One thing surprised him, however; his dog did not seem anxious to go in pursuit, although it had clearly seen it. The hare was there, cornered against the wall. And Jerome put his gun to his shoulder and pulled the trigger: Bang!... The smoke cleared away, and he went forward to pick up his quarry, with no other fear than he might have blown it to bits by shooting from such close quarters. But he was stupefied to find the animal just as alive as before, and it was looking at him motionless, with eyes like a man's.

'There must be a curse on me!' exclaimed Jerome, believing he must have missed, when he was considered as one of the best shots in the land.

And he took aim a second time.

But the hare spoke to him:

'You shouldn't be angry with yourself, for you didn't miss me.'

Jerome was so scared that his gun fell from his hands. The animal went on, in a sad voice:

'Shoot anyway. You'll shorten my penitence; I've still to receive more than seven hundred shots before deliverance.'

Jerome Lhostis picked up his gun, but, as you might well believe, it was to flee as quickly as possible. This time, it was the hare who chased the hunter."

(Told by Marguerite Phillipe, Pluzunet.)

The 'Anaon.'

Don't cry too much over the dead.

"About sixty years ago, fourteen men, including my Uncle Ewan, were drowned off the coast. They had been cutting seaweed and they were bringing it back on a badly-tied raft which came apart.

Their bodies were recovered all together, and placed in a wagon to be brought to the little cemetery where they were all buried in the same grave.

Ewan's wife, my aunt, was so struck by this unhappy event that she went crazy. She no longer ate, drank, nor slept. It was impossible to keep her in the house. At all hours of the day or night, rain or fine, she ran along the beaches, the rocks and the dunes, crying to the echos:

'Ewan, where are you. Ewan, where are you?'

They had to run after her and strike her before she would agree to go back home. One morning when it was scarcely light she had managed to escape again, and she immediately started her eternal cry:

'Ewan, where are you?'

Suddenly she heard what was clearly her dead husband's voice, replying rudely:

'Here!'

She became sane straight away, and, turning towards the direction from where the voice came, she saw him standing before her, dressed as he was on his last day, and exactly as they had dragged him from the water, except that his hair and clothing were no longer dripping wet. She wanted to throw herself in his arms, but he made a sign for her to stop.

'Look,' he said, 'my clothes have had time to dry; now it's your turn to dry your tears.'

And as she was taken aback and unable to find a word in reply, he added:

'Marie, look after what's inside your house and don't busy yourself with what's outside.'

My aunt took him at his word. She moderated her mourning and, by dint of effort, managed to live in peace."

(Told by Claude L'Ollivier, Port-Blanc.)

Chapter 13. Ghosts.

The story of Marie-Job.

"Marie-Job was commission agent for the big island which the Bretons call the 'Enes-Veur.' Every Thursday she went to the market at Lannion in an ageing wagon drawn by a poor old nag. As for the harness, which was in a worse state than the horse, it was, as they say, all done up with string. It was a miracle that the old woman and her team did not break down twenty times on the mud and rock-strewn road which linked the island with the mainland at low tide. It was an even greater miracle, because Marie-Job always crossed in the dark, setting off before dawn, and coming back by moonlight, when there was any. It was equally a miracle that she had never encountered any bad types, for there was no shortage of unscrupulous beachcombers who would have been tempted by the merchandise she carried in her wagon.

They would sometimes ask her:

'Marie-Job, aren't you afraid when you travel all alone at night?'

To which she would reply:

'On the contrary, it's the others who are afraid of me. With the noise my wagon makes, they think it's the Ankou.'

And it is true that, in the dark, one could mistake it from the way its axle squeaks, and the other-worldly look of the horse. And then, if I must tell everything, there was another reason which Marie-Job would not mention herself; it was that she had the reputation of being something of a witch. She knew the 'secrets,' and even the worst rogues preferred to keep their distance rather than risk her curses.

One night, however, she had the following adventure:

It was winter; towards the end of December. It had been freezing enough to break the tombstones since the beginning of the week. Marie-Job had said that if it stayed so cold she would definitely not go to the market at Lannion, not because of herself, but for the sake of Mogis, her horse, which was, as she said, her 'only family.' But it happened that the tobacconist, her best client, came to see her on the Wednesday evening, saying:

'Marie-Job, what's this they're saying; that you're not going to market tomorrow?'

'How could I have a clear conscience if I took Mogis outside in this weather, when even the sea-gulls aren't showing themselves?'

Ghosts.

'I'm asking you this favour for my sake. You know I've always paid you well. Please don't refuse me. I've almost run out of chewing tobacco. If I don't have some more for Sunday, what will I say to the quarrymen when they all come to buy their week's supply?'

I forgot to explain that the 'Enès-Veur' is an island of quarrymen; there are at least three or four hundred of them who work the rock into dressed stone, and they are not always agreeable, as well you might think, especially as there are as many Normans as Bretons amongst them. The tobacconist was certainly not wrong in worrying, for they were types who would wreck her shop, the only one on the island, if she did not have what they wanted. Marie-Job knew this also, for it was she who brought the tobacco every Thursday, and in truth she was upset that this would cause trouble for her best client. But on the other hand, there was Mogis, poor dear Mogis!.... And then she had a foreboding that even for herself, it would not be good to go. A voice inside her kept saying: 'Don't change your mind; you've decided not to go, and you should stay!'

The other, however, kept on begging her, until at last, Marie-Job, who was blunt in her ways, but sensitive inside, said:

'All right; you'll have your tobacco.'

And she went straight to the stable to groom Mogis, as she always did the evening before a journey.

Next day, she left the island at low tide, dressed as usual with her red mittens on her hands and her cape over her shoulders, crying 'gee up' to Mogis who was feeling the wind in his ears like icy needles. Neither the old woman, nor her old horse, felt on form, but nevertheless they reached Lannion without problems. Marie Job parked her wagon by the Silver Anchor inn. When she had collected all her goods, the innkeeper's wife said:

'You can't be thinking of going back! Don't you realise you'll be frozen stiff before you reach the island?'

And she tried to persuade her to sleep there. But the old woman was adamant:

'I'll go back just as I came. Just give me a cup of hot coffee, and a glass of brandy.'

All the same, they could see that she was not looking her best. As she was leaving the Silver Anchor, she said sadly to the innkeeper's wife:

'I think it's going to be a hard trip back. I can hear something bad in my left ear...'

But that did not prevent her from touching Mogis with the whip and setting out into the falling December night. All went well for a time, except that it became colder and colder and Marie-Job felt her body and mind going numb. To keep herself awake she took the reins in one hand, and her rosary in the other, and began reciting aloud. But even her own voice began to make her sleepy, so that despite her efforts she ended up asleep or unconscious. Suddenly, in her torpor, she felt that something was amiss. She rubbed her eyes, roused her thoughts, and realised that the wagon had stopped.

'What's up, Mogis,' she grumbled.

Mogis twitched his ears but did not move.

She touched him with the whip, and still he did not move. Then she struck him with its handle. His spine bent under the blows, but he remained immovable. He was panting for breath and two jets of steam could be seen coming from his nostrils, for it was a clear starry night.

'This is something new,' thought Marie-Job.

For the seventeen years they had been living together, as she put it, Mogis had been exemplary, doing only what his mistress wished. What could have made him behave unexpectedly like this, especially when he had as much reason to hurry to the warmth of his stable as Marie-Job had to her bed? Somewhat reluctantly, she decided to climb down and find out. She expected to find some obstacle, a drunkard perhaps, lying across the road. But search as she may, she found nothing unusual. The road was deserted; she could see only the shadows of the oaks growing on the banks.

'Let's go, Mogis,' said the old woman, to encourage him.

And she grabbed hold of the bridle. The horse snorted loudly, shook its head, and braced its fore-legs, refusing to budge an inch.

Then Marie-Job understood that there must be something supernatural holding them up. As I have told you, she was something of a witch. Anyone else in her place would have been seized with terror. But she knew what to do in all circumstances, and she drew a cross on the road with her whip, saying:

'By this cross which I trace with my bread-winner, I order whatever is here, which I cannot see, to declare if it is here on God's or the Devil's behalf.'

No sooner had she said this, than a voice replied from the

bottom of the ditch:

'It's what I'm carrying that stops your horse from going past.'

She walked bravely towards the voice, holding her whip against her neck, and she saw a little old man, very old, crouching in the grass, looking quite worn out. He looked so weary, so sad, so wretched, that she felt pity for him:

'What on earth are you thinking of, old man, sitting there on such a night as this, risking your death of cold?'

'I'm waiting for a sympathetic soul to help me up,' he replied.

Whatever you are, body or spirit, Christian or Pagan, it won't be said that you lacked Marie-Job's help,' murmured the good woman as she leaned over the wretched one.

With her help, he managed to get on his feet, but his back stayed bent as if it were under an invisible load. Marie-Job asked him:

'What is it you're carrying, that's able to terrify animals?'

The little old man replied in a plaintive tone:

'Your eyes can't see it, but your horse's nose has smelt it. Animals know more about this than men do. Yours will only go on its way when it senses that I'm neither on the road behind it, nor in front of it.

'You don't expect me to stay here indefinitely? I need to get to the island. I've helped you; now it's your turn to advise me: What else must I do?'

'I've no right to ask for anything; it's for you to offer.'

For the first time in her life, Marie-Job was not sure what to do.

'Neither behind him, nor in front of him, on the road' she thought. 'How do we sort that one out?'

Suddenly she exclaimed:

'Once in my wagon, you'll no longer be on the road. Climb up!'

'God bless you!' said the little old man. 'You've worked it out.'

And he dragged himself, all bent over, towards the wagon where he had great trouble in climbing up, even though Marie-Job was pushing him with both hands. When he let himself down on the only seat, it seemed as if the axle bent and there was a sound of creaking planks. The good woman managed somehow to install herself alongside this strange companion, and Mogis trotted off with a greater will than usual, greater even than when he scented his stable.

79

'Then you're going to the island too?' Marie-Job asked him, trying to break the silence.

'Yes,' said the old man, who did not seem to want to chat, and who remained doubled over, no doubt from the weight of his mysterious invisible load.

'I don't remember having seen you before.'

'No, you were too young when I left.'

'It seems you've come a long way.'

'A very long way.'

Marie-Job did not dare question him further. Moreover, they were crossing to the island and she had to pay careful attention because of the mud and rocks on the track which served as a road. Marie-Job did not fail to notice that her wagon wheels dug deeper than usual into the sand.

'We must be heavily loaded,' she muttered beneath her breath.

As she had brought very little from Lannion, and the old man could not weigh much more than a child, she had to conclude that it was the load he claimed to be carrying that weighed so heavy. This gave her something to think about, and perhaps Mogis too, who was beginning to weaken and was stumbling at every step. When they finally reached the Enès-Veur, he was covered in sweat.

There, the road forks. The one on the left goes towards the parish church of Saint Sauveur; the one on the right to the town where Marie-Job had her dwelling. Mogis had stopped, no doubt to recover his wind. She was anxious to be parted from her silent companion, and took the opportunity to say:

'Here we are at the island, old chap; God guide you on your way.'

'Very well,' groaned the little old man.

And he tried to get up, but he quickly fell back on the seat, if not from his own weight, from that of the thing he was carrying. Once again, the axle bent and there was a sound of creaking planks.

'I'll never do it,' he sighed in a way so sad that Marie-Job was deeply moved.

'Well,' she said, 'although I care for nothing of your manners and wish to go home quickly, tell me if there is anything else I can do for you?'

'Well,' he replied, 'take me to Saint Sauveur's cemetery.'

'To the cemetery? At this hour?...' Marie-Job was about to reply that with all the will in the world she could never do that for him, but Mogis did not give her the chance. He set off to the left, towards Saint Sauveur's, as though he had understood the little old man's words. Marie-Job did not know what to think. When they reached the cemetery they found the gate open, although it was normally kept closed. The strange pilgrim let out a cry of satisfaction.

'You can see that I'm expected,' he said; 'and to tell the truth, it's none too soon.'

And, showing a vigour that one would never have expected, he jumped nimbly to the ground.

'All the best then,' said Marie-Job, preparing to take her leave.

But she was not yet at the end of her adventure, for she had scarcely added the customary 'till we meet again' when the little old man said:

'Not yet, please!... Seeing that you've come into this place with me, you're not free to leave until I've accomplished my task. If you leave now, the weight I'm carrying will fall on your shoulders.... I'm telling you this for your own sake and because you've been kind to me. Climb down and follow me.'

Marie-Job, as I have said, was not a person to be easily intimidated, but, from the tone of the little old man's voice, she felt it wisest to obey him. She climbed down and left the reins on Mogis' crupper.

'Now,' said the other, 'I need to know where the last-dead of the Pasquiou family is buried.

'Only that?' she replied. 'I went to the funeral. Come!'

She went amongst the tombstones which were clearly visible in the starlight. When she had found the one she was looking for, she said:

'This is it; the cross is quite new; it should bear the name of Jeanne-Yvonne Pasquiou.... My parents forgot to teach me how to read.'

'And I forgot how to; a long time ago. But we're going to see if you're right or not,' replied the little old man.

Having said this, he prostrated himself at the foot of the tomb. And then a terrifying and unbelievable thing happened. The stone turned on its side, just like a box lid, and Marie-Job felt the cold breath of death on her face, and a noise like that of a coffin hitting the bottom came from below. Pale with fright, she murmured: 'God pardon the dead.'

'You've saved two souls in one go,' said her companion.

He was standing upright now, and quite transformed. Now

81

she could see his face for the first time... The nose was missing, and there were two holes where the eyes should be.

'Don't be afraid, Marie-Job,' he said. 'My name is Mathias Carvennec. No doubt you've heard your father speak of me a long time ago, for we were friends in our youth. He came with the others from the isle to send Patrice Pasquiou and myself off, when we were called up for military service. It was at the time of Old Napoleon. We were both in the same regiment. Patrice was struck by a ball whilst he was next to me; in the ambulance, he said: "I'm going to die; here's all my money; make sure they bury me somewhere easy to recognise, so that if you survive, you'll be able to take my bones to the island and bury them close to my father's." He gave me a considerable sum, at least six hundred francs. I paid for them to bury him in a separate grave, but, when several months later they told us the war had ended and we would be sent home, I was so happy that I forgot about Patrice's request; I went home without him, despite having given him my promise. During the interval my parents had moved from the island to a farm on the mainland, and I went there to join them. I was married there, had children, and died there fifteen years ago. But I was no sooner in my grave than I had to get up. I had no right to rest until I had paid my debt to my friend. I had to go and fetch Pasquiou; I've been walking now for fifteen years between sunset and cock-crow. On even nights I've been walking backwards for three-quarters of the distance I've covered on the odd ones. Patrice's coffin weighed on my shoulders as heavy as the whole tree from which they cut its planks. That's what you heard when there was a sound of creaking planks. Without your help, and your horse's too, I'd have taken another year to get here. Now I've accomplished it. God will reward you, Marie-Job. Go home in peace, and tomorrow put all your affairs in order; for this will have been the last journey for both you and Mogis. See you soon!'

He had scarcely uttered these words when Marie-Job found herself alone amongst the tombs. The ghost had disappeared. The church clock rang midnight. The poor woman felt very cold; she hurried to her wagon and at last reached home. Next day, when the tobacconist came to collect her goods, she found Marie-Job in bed:

'Are you ill, then?' she asked with concern.

'I'm about to die,' replied Marie-Job. 'It's because of you, but I've lived long enough and I've no regrets. All I ask of you is to send me a priest.'

She died the same day. After they had buried her, they had to do the same for Mogis; he was stone cold when they went to look in his stable."

(Told by Anette, a beggar-woman from La Clarté.)

- § -

The ghost's fiancée.

René Pennek was the best looking peasant boy for miles around, and Dunvel Karis, his sweetheart, was the prettiest girl. The two had loved one another since they were quite young. They both came from good families; the only difference being that the Pennecks were twice as rich as the Karis family. Because of this, René's father opposed his son's leaning towards Dunvel. On the other side, Dunvel's father had a proud nature and nothing in the world would make him take the first step towards René's father whom he regarded as his equal or even less, precisely because he felt inferior to him with respect to wealth.

None of this prevented the two young ones from making dates and meeting whenever there was a fair, a ceremony, or any other public gathering.

They seemed to be made for each other, and people were pleased to see them together.

Often they would ask jokingly:

'When's the wedding?'

Dunvel would blush and reply sadly:

'When it pleases God.'

But René would affirm:

'What's sure, is that there'll be one, despite all and everyone.'

Things had been going on like that until, one morning, René's father said to him:

'I've hired some workers to cut down the beeches on our land at Mézou-Meur. I want you to go and supervise them, so they'll get on with the job.'

René Penneck obeyed his father at once. He went to the stable, saddled the stallion, which was the best trotter in the land, and set out on his journey.

To reach the Mézou-Meur, René had a good four leagues to cover, and, at the time I am speaking of, the roads were not like they are today. For the first part of his journey, the road was nothing but holes; the second part up the mountain was on paths which were like the beds of torrents, and the descent on the other side was even more dangerous than the ascent.

'It's going to take all day,' said René to himself as he sat in the saddle.

By that, he meant that it was going to be a whole day without seeing his sweetheart.

To put his mind at rest, he made a detour via the Keris' home. Dunvel was busy spreading the washing out on the grass to dry. René took her in his arms, and then went on his way, whistling a happy refrain. As for Dunvel, it seems she was sad throughout the rest of the day, without knowing the reason why.

The sun was high when René Pennek reached Mezou-Meur. Up till then, his journey had been without problems and the stallion had behaved perfectly. It was not the same, alas, at the end of his journey. The closer he came to the place where they were felling the trees, the more he had to grip his horse's flanks with his legs, and pull in the reins. The sound of the axes chopping into the wood made the horse prick his ears. Suddenly, a beech fell across the road just in front of them. The stallion reared up. René Pennek fell; he fell so unfortunately that his head struck a rock and he was killed outright.

The workers ran towards him. They used branches to make an improvised stretcher for him. The poor young man was taken to the cloggers' hut; the cloggers were there because they had bought the timber from his father.

They borrowed a wagon from the nearest farm, and then they drew lots to see who would have to take his body back home to his parents, for none of them wanted to be the bearer of bad news.

It was nightfall when René Pennek returned home, feet first.

That night, all the Keris family had gone to bed as usual. They had received no news of the unfortunate accident. Dunvel, however, could not sleep at all. She was tossing and turning in bed as though she was being devoured by fleas. Lovers often have presentiments. She kept asking herself why René had not called to say goodnight on his way back, as he had promised. Surely he must have returned hours ago.

Whilst she was reproaching him in her mind for not having kept his promise, she suddenly felt happy:

Ghosts.

She had just heard the sound of a horse's hoofs on the courtyard paving, followed by three vigorous knocks on the door.

No doubt about it; it was him; it was René!

Right then, the clock struck midnight.

Dunvel waited until the clock had finished striking, before answering the knock.

'Is that you, René?' she said.

'Of course it's me!'

'I'm glad you've called to say good night. I was beginning to think you'd let me down, and the thought of it was upsetting me. Now that I've heard your voice, I'll be able to go to sleep.'

'It's no time to think of sleeping. I've come to take you home with me, and make you my wife.'

'What are you dreaming of, René? Don't you know what time it is?'

'What does the time matter? Any time's my time. Get up, Dunvel, and come with me.'

'Then your parents have consented?'

'They can't refuse me now, not any more. Hurry, if you don't want me to become tired of waiting.'

Dunvel got up, but such a thing at so late an hour seemed strange to her. Before opening the door to René Pennek, she went barefoot to her mother's bed and woke her gently to ask her advice.

Mothers are always happy to marry their daughters well. Dunvel's mother deplored her husband's pride which, more than the Pennek's wealth, was the main obstacle to her daughter's happiness. She said to her daughter:

'If René Pennek's come for you in the middle of the night, it's because he's finally got his parents' consent and he's intent on acting whilst the iron's still hot. Go with him, now that he's asked you. Don't turn your back on your lucky star.'

'But don't you have to be there, and my father too?'

'Don't worry about anything. I'm going to prepare your father for the news, which he'll receive gladly, although he won't like admitting it. You go on ahead with René.'

Dunvel did not wait to be told a second time. Her mother had reassured her. She dressed quickly, taking her clogs in one hand, and drawing the bolt back with the other.

'At last! Then you've made up your mind!' exclaimed the voice of René Pennek.

Dunvel's mother waited till she heard the horse gallop

away into the distance, before tugging her husband's shoulder. He was sleeping next to her; the heavy sleep of those who have worked hard in the fields all day.

Her husband was pleased by the news, just as she had predicted. He eagerly put on his best clothes and set out, in the company of his wife who was dressed also in her Sunday best, for the Penneks'. The cowherd went in front holding a lantern, for the night was as black as a mortal sin.

When they were near the Penneks', they saw the whole ground floor was lit up. Surely they were going to have a party. They must only be waiting for them to sign the contract, and then the festivities would begin.

When they crossed the threshold, they were taken aback, for they were reciting the litanies for the dead.

They saw the body of René Penneck laid out on the kitchen table, on a white sheet which reached to the floor. He had a hole in the middle of his forehead, and his brains were showing through it. There was a branch of box on a plate at the lower end of the bed. The plate contained the holy-water they sprinkle on the dead. His father and mother were weeping silently at either side of the hearth.

Dunvel's parents did not dare ask a question.

The same thought had occurred to each of them. René Pennek had been killed on his way back from their house.

But what had happened to Dunvel?

In vain they looked amongst the kneeling women who were saying the funeral prayers.

This is what had happened to her:

René Pennek, or, if you prefer, his ghost, had taken her behind him on the crupper. His horse had gone like the wind. This horse had such a long tail that it whipped her across the face, drawing blood from her cheeks, so that Dunvel cried:

'René, my love, don't you think we're going too fast?'

But René Penneck only replied:

'We must go, my sweetheart! We must go!'

'René, my love, are we going the right way?'

'Any way, my sweetheart, leads where we must go.'

'René, my love, does this road lead to your parents'?'

'I'm taking you to my home, sweetheart. Don't you want that as much as I do?'

Such were the words they exchanged during the night.

Dunvel suddenly saw a large black object rise before her; it was the town church. The cemetery gates were wide open. The horse went along the main alley, leapt over four or five graves in a single bound, and stopped by a freshly-dug grave.

Before she knew what was happening, Dunvel was lying at the bottom of the hole.

'This is our wedding-bed,' said René Pennek, and he lay on top of her...

Next day, when the grave diggers were ready to bury René Pennek, they drew back in horror. The disfigured and flattened body of Dunvel was lying at the bottom of the grave."

(Told by Francoise Omnès, Bégard, 1890.)

- § -

The lighthouse ghost.

"I used to be the one and only keeper of the lighthouse at Tévennec. It was built on a rock which was only just big enough to take its foundations. The life I led was not very exciting. Apart from the provisioner who brought oil for the lamp, and food for myself every eight days, weather permitting, there were no other visitors. When he unloaded the provisions on my narrow platform, we would have but a brief conversation:

'Hello.'

'Hello boss.'

'All right?'

'All right.'

'Then, till the next time.'

'Till the next time.'

And I would go back into my prison where I heard nothing but the sound of the waves, the roar of the wind, and the cries of passing birds, sometimes as the latter crashed into the lantern's lighted windows... There were, however, times when I heard strange noises from the inside of the light-house; noises which made me think I was not the only in-habitant of the place. Sometimes there was the sound of footsteps above my head, on the floor of the room I used in the daytime; sometimes a feeling of someone invisible in the shadows on the staircase when I was going up to light the lamp; sometimes there would be a sudden calling of my name, which would make me jump:

'Henri... Eh! Henri...'

Ghosts.

The first few times I heard this call, I would reply:
'What? Who's there?'
And I would go down the steps four at a time to the little
platform, to see if it were some fisherman I knew who was
passing by and wanted to exchange a few words. But there
was never anyone there, although I loooked everywhere. At
length, I stopped paying attention to these calls, and to the
other strange noises which had worried me at first. Born
and bred as I was on the 'Ile de Sein,' I was well aware of
the doleful stories they told about Tévennec. From further
back than one can remember, this rock of shipwrecks has
been considered as a place haunted by the ghosts of those
drowned at sea. Before the lighthouse was built, they said
the ghosts on the rock were as numerous as the cormorants
which rested there. There is one tale that cannot be denied;
that of a ship which sank close to Tévennec and from which
a single survivor managed to climb on to the rock. For four
days and nights he cried for help, but they were unable to
rescue him because of the heavy seas. When it was calm
enough for them to reach the rock, his body had disappeared
but there remained a blood-stain in a hollow of the rock
which has never disappeared. His soul continued to haunt
the place where he died, and, after they built the lighthouse
the general belief was that his ghost was enclosed within it.

I tried to make myself believe that the noises were due
to his ghost, and, from the time when his presence ceased
to trouble me, I began to ignore him, and never said anything of this to my family when I was on leave.

We had been getting on all right, the ghost and I, when,
at the end of one of my leaves, my wife's cousin offered to
come to the lighthouse and spend eight days with me. At
that time the rules and regulations about that sort of thing
were not so strict as they are now. I took this cousin back
with me, and we installed ourselves in my room, with the
idea of passing the time as well as possible. All went well
for the first three days, but, at the end of the third day,
just as we were enjoying an excellent after-dinner coffee,
the ghost started a performance on the floor above us. This
time, it was not content just walking to and fro in its boots;
it seemed to be playing the carpenter as well, with sounds
like sawing and planing wood. The cousin listened, quite
bewildered.

'What's that?' he asked, when he had recovered from the
shock.

'Oh, don't be surprised,' I said. 'He's done very well to keep quiet till now.'

'Who's he?'

'Someone who seems to know me, for he often calls me by my name, although he's never told me what he calls himself.'

'And is he in the habit of making such a row?'

'Almost every night.'

'He's a strange fellow, truly he is.'

'I think he's more a ghost than a fellow.'

'Brr! You're making me go cold all over.'

'In that case, you'd better warm yourself up with this.'

I poured a good measure of brandy into his coffee, which warmed him up and roused his courage. He started cracking jokes and, as the noise above increased, he said with a somewhat quizzical laugh:

'You don't know? If I were in your shoes, I'd invite him down to have a drink with us. At least like that he'd be quieter, and perhaps tell us his story when a good drink had loosened his tongue.'

The cousin had scarcely finished speaking when the ghost also became suddenly silent.

'See,' he went on, 'it only needed my proposition to calm him down. Why don't you go; you won't have to beg him for long before he accepts.'

I had never thought of such a thing, and if I had, I would never have had the sacrilegious audacity to go through with it. But the cousin was there; I did not want him to think I was afraid, and, without further thought, I rushed upstairs.

The floor where the noise usually came from was the one reserved for the engineer of Bridges and Highways, when he came on his tour of inspection. I had the key on me; I put it in the lock and, with the door open, I took two or three steps into the darkness of the room, which was black as a tomb. Nothing moved, but, since going in, I had felt a damp breath on my face, a breath faintly impregnated with the smell of death; it made me go cold all over. I had to clear my throat before I could speak:

'Whoever you are, show yourself, and give pleasure to two Christians who are inviting you to come down and drink with them.'

'Bravo!' cried the cousin from below.

As for the ghost's reply, I don't even know if there was one, for, as soon as I had spoken the last word, I received such a blow in the middle of my chest that I was knocked down as though by a thunderbolt. I lost consciousness for I don't know how long; all I know is that it was after midnight when I came round, and all my limbs were aching as though they had been beaten hour after hour. I could not stand up, and I went out backwards on all fours. Back in my room, the lamp was flickering on the table; I looked for the cousin but the only trace left of him was his glass which he had not emptied, something quite out of character for him. I called him five or six times. At last, a head bathed in a sweat of fear came from under the bed and, a moment later, he was in full view.

'He didn't chop you to bits?' he asked, breathing heavily.

'Not quite, but almost. Could you hear him?'

'I'd have had to be stone deaf not to have heard him; it sounded like twenty blows at a time and the tower was shaking on its foundations; I thought it was going to collapse and I hid under the bed so I wouldn't see death approaching.

'Well let's get to bed now,' I groaned; 'I can't take any more of this.'

Next morning I was surprised my hair had not turned white. Fifteen days later, I had given in my resignation. The ghost of Tévennec had put me off ever being a lighthouse keeper again."

(Told by Henri Porzmoguer, Ile de Sein.)

Chapter 14. Exorcism.

The people that need to be exorcised are almost always the rich who have obtained their wealth by wicked means, and those who have led a disorderly life. Therefore they are mostly nobles and bourgeois; peasants have too hard a task earning their living not to be peaceful after their death.

- § -

Their souls are condemned to wander until all the wrongs they have done have somehow been put right. They are ill-tempered and wicked. They prowl about their old home, and get their own back for their distress by making trouble amongst the living. They are exorcised in order to immobilise and silence them.

- § -

Only priests have the power of exorcism. Not all priests can do it. It needs one who has the know-how, ability and determination. It is quite something if there is one in every region. It is not enough for the exorcist to know his science thoroughly; it is also essential that he is a tough character.

- § -

When the priest is called for an exorcism, he puts his surplice on and carries his stole in his hand. He takes his shoes off when he reaches the haunted house, for he must be 'priest right to the ground.'

The evening before his arrival, the people of the house have to sprinkle fine sand or ashes over the floors and steps of the house from the front door right to the attic. This permits the exorcist to follow the the ghost's footsteps and to shut himself in the room where they seem to end. That is where the evil ghost is lying. A terrible combat takes place between the exorcist and the ghost. Sometimes the priest comes back from his encounter worn out, pale, and covered in sweat. During the time this sinister meeting is taking place, the people of the house huddle around the hearth, dumb with fright. They block their ears so as to try not to hear the terrible din coming from the room. They ask themselves who is going to win, the evil ghost or the man of God. Sometimes the priest repeats special prayers; sometimes he struggles bodily with the ghost; sometimes he asks the ghost difficult questions, and takes advantage of the moment the other is busy thinking what to reply, to put his silken stole around its neck. Then the ghost is beaten. It becomes grovelling and docile. The priest says the rite of exorcism over it and makes it enter into an animal's body, most often that of a black dog. He takes it outside the house and entrusts it to someone in his confidence, often the verger or the sacristan, one of whom would often accompany him on such a mission. Then they go, the priest in front, the other one behind and leading the animal, towards some rarely-frequented place, such as a barren heath, a disused quarry, or a quagmire. 'From now on this is where you shall live,' says the priest to the ghost; and he marks out a circle delimiting the space in which it can move; he often uses a barrel hoop for this purpose. They choose a rarely-frequented spot because, if someone were to pass close by, he would surely be grabbed by the feet and dragged underground.

- § -

Tadic-coz, exorcist.

"This took place when Tadic-coz was at Bégard. He was a priest of the old school, a brave old man who was more often to be found on the roads and footpaths than at home. Everyone knew him, from the mountains right to the sea. He had an extraordinary charity of soul and he was very fond of the young and the poor.

I knew him for a long time, and I only knew him as an old man. I have heard them say he was older than the earth; that he had died and been resurrected ten times.

I will describe him for you:

He had an arched back, and long white hair.

One could not be sure whether his face was that of an old man or a child. He was always laughing and joking.

His cassock was made from patches, but there were more holes than patches in it.

Every morning, after mass, he would go on his rounds. When he met anyone, he always began the conversation in the same way:

'Tell me how you are, my child. I'm your father, your little old father.'

That is why they always called him Tadic-coz (little old

Exorcism.

father, or old daddy).

They loved him, and they venerated him; but they feared
him as well; for not only was he a good priest; he was also
a learned one, one to whom God, they said, had given as
much power as the Pope.

Tadic-coz knew many things; about all the secrets of life
and all the secrets of death. They said that, from time to
time, he leant his head over the pit of hell to talk with the
devils. He had no equal when it came to saying the 'ofern
drantel.' They came from all over Brittany to consult him,
and even from France. When he could not save a soul, he at
least managed to make it rest in peace. There has never
been anyone as good at exorcism as Tadic-coz.

I am now going to tell you a tale about this, which I have
from the very person to whom it happened:

He was a soldier, stationed at Lyons, a long way from
here.

Having obtained a month's leave, he wanted to show himself in uniform to his own people, and he took the stage
coach to Brittany. (This was before the time of the rail-
ways). The coach dropped him at Belle-Isle-en-Terre. From
there, he still had a good three leagues to go to his village;
but what is three leagues to a soldier on leave!

He started walking.

As he was passing the Ménez-Bré, he saw an old priest
walking with difficulty, quite bent over and leading a black
dog, a horrible beast.

'Hello there,' cried the soldier when he saw him coming.
'It's Tadic-coz, good old Tadic-coz! Good day, Tadic-coz.'

'Good day, my child.'

'Then you don't recognise me, Tadic-coz?'

'That's because my sight's failing, my child.'

'I'm Jobic, Jobic Ann Drez. It was you who baptised me.'

'Yes, yes, I remember; your mother will be very pleased
to see you....' And, after a moment of hesitation, the old
priest added: 'No doubt you're in a hurry to get home?'

'That I am, Tadic-coz. I shan't be sorry to get there. But
why did you ask me that?'

'Because... If you'd had the time... There's this villain of a
dog that I've to take to the vicar of Louargat... And my legs
are so old they're wobbling under me... To tell the truth,
I don't know if I've the strength to go that far.'

My friend Jobic felt his heart move with pity. Moreover,
poor Tadic-coz really did look worn out.

93

Exorcism.

'All right, I'll do it for you, and only for you, Tadic-coz.
Give me the dog's lead. I'll take it to the vicar of Louargat.
It means going the opposite way, but it doesn't matter! No
one refuses Tadic-coz a favour. You can go back home and
leave it to me. If you meet any of my family on the way,
please tell them I'll be there before nightfall.'
'Bless you, my child!'
And Tadic-coz gave Jobic the black dog's lead.
The hideous beast started growling, but Tadic-coz silenced
it by muttering some latin words, and it followed its new
leader quietly.
Half an hour later, Jobic reached Louargat and knocked on
the vicar's door.
'Here's the dog Tadic-coz asked me to bring you.'
The vicar gave Jobic a strange look.
'Did you volunteer for this?'
'Of course; just to please Tadic-coz.'
'Well then, my child, you're not yet at the end of your
troubles.'
'What do you mean by that?'
'You'll see... Have a glass of wine whilst you're waiting;
you'll need to rest your legs before walking as far as Belle-
Isle.'
'What! To Belle-Isle!' exclaimed Jobic.'You must be joking!
Here's your dog; keep it; do whatever you want with it. As
for me, I'm off home! But for Tadic-coz, I'd be there by
now. Good day and good-bye, vicar!'
'Steady on, my boy. Once you take charge of one of these
dogs, you can't just drop them anywhere you like. If you
were unfortunate enough to let go of this dog, you'd be
finished. Your soul would be condemned to take the place
of the evil one that's in it; just think whether you'd like
that or not.'
'Then it's not really a dog,' muttered Jobic, who had suddenly become mild, and even lost some of his colour.
'No it's not! It's some evil ghost that Tadic-coz must have
exorcised. Look at it's eyes!'
Jobic looked closely at the dog for the first time; he
saw that it's eyes were extraordinary, like the devil's.
'It's a dirty trick Tadic-coz has played on me; but it
doesn't matter...'
'Now that you're in it,' said the vicar, 'the best you can
do is go on to the end.'
'Then I'll have to go to Belle-Isle, now?'

94

Exorcism.

'Yes, and you should tell my counterpart there that it was I who sent you.'

'I'll be off now, seeing there's no choice,' said Jobic with a sigh.

And he set off to Belle-Isle, going back over the ground he had covered a few hours earlier. He had been singing happily then, but now he was as sad as could be.

The vicar of Belle-Isle gave him a warm reception.

'My boy,' he said, 'you can sleep here tonight, and continue your journey tomorrow.'

'Then this dog's not really for you, either?' asked Jobic.

'No, my friend.'

This time Jobic felt like going into a rage, but his eyes met those of the accursed dog, and he dropped into a chair and burst into tears.

'And just to think,' he sobbed, 'that by now I could have been sitting at my parents' kitchen table.'

'Console yourself,' said the vicar. 'I don't intend to let you die of starvation. Give me the lead, and I'll lock the dog in the cellar. You can have some supper and a good night's sleep.'

As he had not eaten all day, Jobic ate with relish, despite his sadness, and, when he went to bed, he slept like a log. Next morning the vicar himself came to wake him.

'Get up, friend! The sun's already shining. The dog's howling! It's time to be off! Try your best to reach the vicarage at Gurunhuël in time for lunch, and tell the vicar that I sent you.'

And Jobic moved out. What else could he do? He had to submit to what he could not prevent.

We will not follow him in detail from vicarage to vicarage.

The vicar of Gurunhuël sent him to the one of Callac.

The vicar of Callac to the one of Maël-Carhaix.

The vicar of Maël-Carhaix to... etc., etc...

In two days he visited a dozen vicarages, warmly welcomed at each one; everywhere he found good food, wine, and lodging.

It annoyed him all the same, at first because he thought his strange journey would never come to an end, and later because he began to become an object of curiosity to the people he passed by, who seemed intrigued by the sight of a soldier leading a dog.

Towards midday of the third day he reached the vicarage at Commana, high up on the Monts d'Aré.

Exorcism.

'With respect sir, here's a dog...'

It was the thirteenth or fourteenth time he had spoken these words. He had reached the stage of saying them in a pitiful tone, like someone begging alms.

The vicar of Comanna interrupted him:

'I know, I know. Help yourself to a glass of cider in the kitchen. I want you to be on form to give me a hand shortly, for this animal doesn't look very pleasant.'

'Have no fear,' said Jobic. 'I'll willingly help, if it's to be rid of it at last.'

'Be ready as soon as I give you the word; but we'll have to wait till sunset...'

'And about time,' thought Jobic; 'this is a language I can understand.'

To tell the truth, he did not understand very much, for the hardest part was still to come; but then he would be free.

The vicar called him at sunset.

The latter was wearing his surplice and carrying his stole.

'Let's go,' he said. 'Above all, take care it doesn't escape; otherwise we'll both be lost.'

'Don't worry,' said Jobic, winding the rope round his fist.

They set out, all three of them; the vicar walking in front, then Jobic, and finally the dog.

They went to a big dark mountain, much higher and wilder than the Ménez-Bré. The earth was black all around them, and there was neither grass, heather, nor moss.

When they reached the foot of the mountain, the vicar stopped for a moment:

'We are going into the bog,' he said. 'Whatever you hear, don't look round, or you'll lose your life in this world and your salvation in the next. Is the animal secure?'

'Yes, yes, vicar.'

It was a sorry place they went to; desolation on desolation; black earth sodden with black water.

'This must be the entrance to hell,' said Jobic to himself.

No sooner were they in this quagmire than the dog began howling pitifully, struggling in a frenzy; but Jobic did not let go.

The further they went, the more the accursed dog leapt and howled. It pulled so hard on the rope that Jobic's hands were bleeding.

No matter; he still held on.

Now they were in the middle of the bog.

Exorcism.

'Take care!' whispered the vicar in Jobic's ear.

He went up to the dog and, just as the latter was about to bite him, with great dexterity slipped his stole around its neck. The animal uttered a terrible cry; it was a cry of lamentable sadness.

'Quick! Lie face-down on the ground,' said the vicar, doing likewise himself.

Jobic had scarcely prostrated himself when he heard the sound of a body falling in the water, followed immediately by hissing noises and explosions; in fact, a terrible din. He could have sworn the swamp was on fire.

It lasted half an hour; then all became quiet again.

Then the vicar of Commana said to Jobic:

'You can go back now, the way you came; but don't forget to call at each of the vicarages you visited on your way here. You should tell each vicar that the mission has been accomplished.

Jobic needed no persuasion this time, and he set out on the road.

He sang all along the way, happy he was no longer leading the dog, and happy to be on his way home.

He went from vicarage to vicarage, until at last he came to the one at Louargat.

'Ah! There you are, my boy!' said the vicar. 'Good! Now you should go and find Tadic-coz; he's anxious to see you.'

Tadic-coz! Jobic felt his anger coming back as soon as he heard this name. He would certainly go and see this Tadic-coz, and use the opportunity to tell him what he thought of him.

However it was Tadic-coz who told him something which astonished him.

Guess who Jobic had taken to the bog?

It was his own grandfather.

Since he had died several months earlier, his family and the others around had had nothing but trouble.

They had asked Tadic-coz to use his science to find out the cause of the trouble.

And so Jobic, after having been hoaxed by the old priest, found himself still in his debt."

(Told by Baptiste Geffroy, Penvénan, 1886.)

- § -

97

Exorcism.

The red dress.

There was a rich heiress in the town of Plogonnec. She was called Marie-Jean Pérennou. She was much sought after, and eventually she agreed to marry Joseph Rumeur from the village of Kerlestr, and they fixed the wedding-day.

At that time the young women of the land were married in red. Marie-Jean had a magnificent red dress made, embroidered with gold flowers and braided with silver. Vanity was her weakness; she had been told about this more than once. When the wedding-day arrived, all the parish lined up to see the procession and admire the heiress in her incomparable dress; and they exclaimed 'Oh!' and 'Ah!' as they went by. But the old folks shook their heads, saying:

'When one makes oneself so beautiful to start married life, it's sure one hasn't long to live happily.'

And the saying came true for Marie-Jean, for, after having given birth to her first child, she was taken with a fever and died in the flower of her youth, to her husband's great sadness, for he adored her. Joseph Rumeur was inconsolable. During the day he worked on the farm, as usual; but in the evening, when his mother - who had come to look after the house - and all the servants were in bed, he would sit in the corner by the hearth hour after hour deploring his sad lot. Sometimes he would cry himself to sleep on the seat by the hearth, with his feet in the ashes.

One night when he had let himself fall asleep like that, he dreamt that the kitchen door opened and his wife came in, all pale and wrapped in a mud-stained shroud. He rubbed his eyes and suddenly realised that what he imagined to be a dream, was not one at all. His wife really was there, in front of him. He saw her go quietly to the cupboard where she kept her clothing when she was alive, turn the key and open the doors, which squeaked on their hinges as she did so. She opened the drawer inside, and took out her wedding dress; her splendid dress which they had religiously folded and put away for ever. She also took out her other wedding adornments. She laid everything out on the bench, and then started to dress.

Her husband watched her do this without saying a word, and without daring to move.

Once dressed, she went in front of the mirror and put her head-dress on. Then he saw her smile at her own reflection, although it was not all that seductive, seeing it was of one who was dead and buried. Then she began to walk across the room.

'She's coming towards me; she's going to speak to me,' said Joseph to himself.

And his heart seemed to leap in his chest.

But when she came near the hearth, she did not even seem to notice if there was anyone there, and, turning on her heels, she walked the other way. She seemed only concerned with her appearance and the way she walked, looking over her shoulder to see if her dress looked well behind her. As she walked to and fro in this way, she kept repeating:

'Don't I look pretty! Aren't I well turned out!'

When it was time for her to go, she undressed as though it were nothing unusual; then she disappeared without having cast even a single glance at the cradle where her child was sleeping. And that upset Joseph even more than the way he had been ignored himself. Next day, he told himself:

'I must see if she comes back tonight.'

And, half to prove he had not been dreaming open-eyed, half because he no longer wished to stay up alone by the hearth, he asked one of his manservants to stay up with him, but without telling him what it was all about. They sat facing one another, drinking several bowls of cider and exchanging a few words. Joseph went off into his usual dreamy thoughts, and the conversation flagged.

'For what good I'm doing here, I'd be better off between the sheets,' said the manservant to himself as he began to feel sleepy.

And the master, who saw he had had enough, said to himself:

'Perhaps she's late in coming because I've a stranger with me.'

He was wrong. The door opened at the stroke of midnight and Marie-Jean came in and repeated her previous night's performance. Once again she was only concerned with admiring herself in her red dress, and she took no notice of the others in the room.

When she had disappeared again, Joseph said to the manservant:

'Well! You saw and heard it all, didn't you?'

'What?' asked the other, startled.

The poor man had been asleep, as could be expected of someone who had worked in the fields all day.

'What?' he repeated again.

'Nothing, nothing, 'replied Joseph, 'except that it's time you went to bed.'

And he wished him good night. But as for himself, he stayed up till dawn, and ran to the church in order to catch the vicar on his way to say mass. The vicar of Plogonnec was a learned man, as familiar with the things of the other world as with this one. He listened to every word Joseph spoke to him.

'Perfect,' he said. 'I'll keep you company tonight. Can you tell me what was your wife's favourite drink?'

'She would willingly have a small glass of brandy whenever we had friends over for a drink on a Sunday evening. She said it was like velvet in her stomach.'

'Good! Have a bottle of brandy and three glasses ready on the table. I'll be there about ten o'clock. But don't tell anyone about this, and don't be surprised by anything I do or say. If you do that, I promise you I'll get to the bottom of it.'

Joseph Rumeur went back home, his mind more at ease. He worked all day in the fields with his workmen, and, as soon as supper was over, sent everyone away. He placed the bottle of brandy and three glasses on the table, just as the vicar had asked. The latter arrived on time, dressed in a surplice and with a black stole around his neck. They sat awake together, frequently glancing at the door. At last, just before midnight, they saw it open, and Marie-Jean appeared. She went straight to the cupboard, took out her red dress and began a repeat of the previous night's performance. She either did not notice the priest, or could not see him in the shadows.

The latter got up and stood in front of the ghost:

'Good day, Marie-Jean!'

'Good day, vicar. Is it really you?'

'Yes, Marie-Jean. I'm here to help you as best I can. How does the other world suit you?'

'But... Well enough..,' she replied hesitantly.

'But it seems to me that you've kept your taste for this world... Wouldn't you like to have a small glass of brandy with us?'

'I wouldn't say no.'

The vicar poured out three glasses. He gave one to the husband, kept the second for himself, and pushed the third one towards the edge of the table.

'Come closer, Marie-Jean, and let's drink.'

Her eyes sparkled when she saw the glass, but she made no movement towards it.

'Pass it to me, vicar,' she begged.

'No. I want you to take it yourself.'

And seeing that she still did not move, he added:

'Perhaps it's not close enough to you.'

He took the glass from the table and put it on the floor, almost at her feet.

'There you are, Marie-Jean. I think it's close enough now.'

'Hand it to me,' she insisted.

'No,' said the vicar. 'As you're being stubborn, I'll be just as stubborn as you.'

Time went by and the ghost, realising it was approaching her time to leave, began to become nervous. She had no doubt that the vicar was planning to do something to her, but on the other hand, she had a great desire for a taste of the drink she had formerly liked so much. In the end, the temptation proved greater than her fear. She leant down to pick up the drink. This was the moment the vicar had been waiting for. Scarcely had she lowered her head than he had imprisoned her in a loop of his stole.

'Got you, Marie-Jean,' he exclaimed.

Then, as he quickly tightened the loop round her neck, he recited some Latin words. She yelled and struggled but, as the priest went on reciting, she slowly changed her form, first into a monster, and finally into a large black dog, - as black as the vicar's cassock.

Joseph Rumeur himself had gone as white as the surplice.

'Go and bring me a rope, and make sure it's strong,' said the priest.

The stole was soon replaced by the rope.

'Now go and tie the dog outside, to one of those rings let in the wall. You can leave it there for the night. Tomorrow you must ask the most willing of your labourers to take it to the last farm on the slopes of the Menez-Aré. The people there will tell him what to do. As for me, my task is accomplished and I wish you good night. Follow my instructions and you'll no longer be tormented by your wife... Above all, see that no one strikes the dog.'

After having said this, the vicar went away.

Next day, when the chief labourer came to ask what work he should do that day, Joseph Rumeur said:

'You should take the dog that's tied up outside, to the Menez-Aré. Go to the last farm before the mountain and

tell them you've come on behalf of the vicar of Plogonnec.
They'll tell you what to do then.'

'Good!' said the labourer.

And having put on his best walking shoes, he set out with
the dog. Joseph Rumeur accompanied him to the edge of his
land.

'Take care not to beat it,' he said as he left him.

All went well for the first few leagues, but when he left
the plain for the mountains, the dog began to drag. The
labourer became impatient and started cursing and swearing:

'Come on, you old carcass.'

And, forgetting his master's advice, he beat the dog, and
the latter began to whine in a human voice:

'Oh Yannic, why did you beat me? Don't you know that
I'm your former mistress, Marie-Jean? You must remember
how good I was to you when I was alive.'

Yannic, the labourer, was so shocked that he almost fell
over backwards. The dog took advantage of this to try and
escape. Fortunately he had taken the precaution to tie the
rope round his wrist.

'You're lucky,' said Marie-Jean, foaming with rage, 'if I'd
managed to get away from you, I'd have finished you off.'

He took her at her word and avoided beating her for the
rest of the journey. He reached the last miserable inhabited
farm just as the sun was going down. There, Yannic was able
to rest and recover a little, eating a piece of larded bread,
for he had had nothing since leaving Plogonnec.

'And what should I do with the animal now,' he asked the
farmer when he had finished eating.

'Oh, don't worry about that. The priest from Saint-Rivoal
is already on his way here,' replied the farmer.

'Someone's been to tell him, then?'

'There's no need. As soon as you left Plogonnec this morning, his books would have told him he would be needed here
tonight.'

Before the farmer had finished speaking, the priest from
Saint-Rivoal arrived at the door.

'Who sent this dog?' he asked.

'The vicar of Plogonnec,' said the boy.

'Good. Go back and tell him I've taken charge of it, and
that I'll do what he intends. But don't speak a single word
to anyone, not even in reply, until you have spoken to him.'

The boy set off home straight away, and he walked all
night.

Exorcism.

'You don't look very happy,' said the vicar of Plogonnec when he saw him.

'Well, I've had to walk more than twenty leagues.'

But the vicar knew well that there was something else he was not telling.

'You beat the dog, didn't you?'

'Yes,' he confessed, lowering his head.

'Well,' said the vicar, 'you got away with it without too much trouble; it could have been much worse for you.'

Joseph Rumeur's labourer was ill for a year; he had lost his taste for food and did not feel well enough to work. In the hiring season of November he told his master he had decided to leave and seek employment elsewhere. And in fact, his bodily and mental health only recovered when he took up work in another place."

(Told by Louise Cosquer, Kerfeunteun.)

- § -

Chapter 15. Hell*.

The road to Hell is wide and well-maintained; it invites the traveller to take it. It has ninety-nine roadside inns** in each of which one must stay for a hundred years. Good-looking, friendly bar staff serve drinks, which taste better and better the closer one is to Hell. If the traveller resists the temptation to drink to excess, and reaches the last inn without being drunk, he is free to go back; Hell has no more hold on him. But in the case of those arriving drunk, they are given a horrible mixture of snake and toad's blood to drink. From then on they belong to the Devil, and are done for.

- § -

The dead never come back from Hell, but there are living souls who have been there and back.

- § -

The Devil's horse.

"One night Jean-René Cuzon was going back to Faou, from the fair at Landernau. The road to Faou is long, and he whistled as he walked, to keep his legs going and keep himself company.

'You whistle marvellously,' said a sudden voice from behind him.

Jean-René turned round and saw a man on horseback.

'Where are you going?' asked the man.

'To Faou.'

'I'm going that way also. We can travel together.'

So they went on, side by side.

'Your horse doesn't make much noise,' said Jean-Rene. 'I'd say it wasn't shod.'

'It's still young and its feet are tender,' replied the unknown one.

* Le Braz also gave a chapter entitled 'Paradise' (Heaven); we have not translated it because the stories in it are too close to ones we have recently published in a section entitled 'Travelling Towards the Sun' in Luzel, 'Celtic Folk-Tales from Armorica.'

**In his chapter entitled 'Paradise,' Le Braz included a tongue-in-cheek tale of ninety-nine inns on the road to Heaven. As one might guess, some Bretons are permanently stuck at the 'Half-Way Inn' because they are always drunk, and incapable of answering when their names are called.

Hell.

The conversation went on amicably.

They talked about the poeple of Faou. The man seemed to know everyone, in the town and its surroundings, from the richest to the poorest. He told very strange tales about each of them: 'Such-a-one is a drunkard..., another, a miser... another beats his wife..., this one's jealous.' And with each name he mentioned, he told a tale to prove his words. He was an amusing companion and Jean-René was delighted to have met him.

Whilst chatting thus, they reached the entrance to an avenue on the left of the road.

'I need to stop here,' said the horseman. 'I've some business at the manor over there, behind the trees. Would you be so kind as to hold my horse's reins? I'll be back soon.'

'Willingly! But I'm afraid you'll be wasting your time. No one will be up at this time of the night.'

'Yes they will. They're expecting me.'

'Go on, then!'

'Make sure the horse doesn't get away.'

'Don't worry. I've held friskier ones than this.'

The horseman jumped down, took the saddle-bag, and off he went.

Jean-René wrapped the reins round his wrist and, as an additional precaution, took a firm grip on the horse's mane.

'You're hurting me,' sighed the horse; 'please don't pull so hard on my mane.'

'What!' said Jean-René. 'Horses are starting to talk now!'

'I'm a horse today, but I was a woman when I was alive. Look at my feet, and you'll see.'

Jean-René looked and saw that the horse really had dainty little feet, like a woman's.

'My God!' he exclaimed, 'then what sort of a man is he?'

'That's not a man; it's the Devil!'

'Oh!'

'He's stopped here to take the soul of a young girl who's just died at the manor. Right now he's putting it in the saddle-bag you saw him take with him, and shortly he'll take her to Hell. You can expect a similar fate if you haven't cleared off before he comes back...'

Jean-René did not wait any longer. He reached Faou out of breath. He could not speak for three days. It was only on the fourth night that he was able to tell his adventure."

(Told by Nanna Gostalen, Le Faou, 1886).

Hell.

Jean Gomper's receipt.

"Jean Gomper was a farmer. He was a capable man, and always paid his quarterly rent on time. The last time he went to pay it, the landlord was not at home. His son was there, however, and Jean Gomper gave him the money, saying: 'I'll see your father at the market. Ask him to give me a receipt then.'

'As you wish,' replied the son.

And Jean Gomper went back home, his mind at ease. Being honest himself, he never doubted anyone's honesty. That is where he went wrong, this time at least, for, two days later, he heard of his landlord's death, and before the week was ended, a man came to see him on the son's behalf to collect the rent.

'But I've paid it!' exclaimed Jean Gomper. 'The son knows all about it, for it was to him that I gave the money.'

'In that case, let me see your receipt. I have to settle the estate; I must do my job properly,' said the man.

Jean Gomper tried to tell him how it had all happened.

'Yap, yap, yap!' said the man, 'show me your receipt, if you have one. I don't take words as payment.'

Jean Gomper, of course, could not produce a receipt.

'If you don't bring the rent to my office during the coming week,' said the man, 'I'll seize all your possessions.'

It was ruin, destitution, for Jean Gomper and his family.

'How can we rid ourselves of this evil?' he howled.

And, in despair, he tore his hair out by the handful.

'God isn't just! No, God isn't just!'

'Why don't you start by asking him?' said his wife. 'If I were in your place, I'd go straight to the vicar. I'm sure he would give some good advice.'

'No one's ever paid the rent with good advice,' groaned Jean Gomper.

All the same, he followed his wife's suggestion.

The vicar was eating his supper, but he was the type who do not like keeping people waiting. Jean Gomper was shown into the dining room. Once there, he explained his case as well as he could, and not without embellishing his story with some swear-words. But the vicar only paid attention to the main point of the story, and, when the peasant had finished, he said:

'You're not lying, Jean Gomper? Is it really true that you have already paid the money they're demanding?'

106

'As true as I'm my wife's legitimate husband, and father to her four children.'

'Then the only thing to do is to go and find the landlord, wherever he is, and ask him for the receipt he didn't give you when he was alive.'

'Hmm!' said Jean Gomper, 'I don't know which way to go for that.'

'I'll show you.'

'I understand you quite well,' continued the farmer, who thought the vicar must be joking. 'Maybe it will be easy enough to go there, but what about coming back?'

'I'll see to that also.'

'Are you serious?'

'You ought to know that a priest never jokes about such things.'

'The vicar had spoken in a serious tone, and the peasant began turning his hat in his hands; murmuring bashfully:

'I'll go wherever you send me, vicar.'

The vicar opened the door of a darkened room, saying:

'First of all I'll go and find out.'

'All right if it's to Heaven,' thought Jean Gomper, 'but that would surprise me. I don't think that rascal of a landlord could be staying in so good a place.'

The vicar had shut himself in the room. The farmer heard him murmuring softly, but quickly, very quickly.

'He's consulting his Red Book,' he said to himself.

When the consultation was ended, the vicar came back:

'You'll have to go to Hell,' he said from the doorway.

Jean Gomper started with fright.

'Will you go?' asked the vicar.

'All right,' replied our man, after a brief hesitation.

The vicar placed his hands on him, used his thumb to trace a cross on his chest, and blew on his forehead:

'Pff!'

Jean Gomper was already at the devil's, and I assure you he had no time to admire the scenery on the way.

Before sending him off thus, the vicar had given him his instructions:

'Take care not to take the first, or the second receipt you are offered. Only the third one will be good. Don't take it from his hands; if you do, you'll be burnt to the marrow, and become a prey to the demons. You must get the landlord to place it on the ground, and then you can pick it up. That way you'll be safe; you'll have kept the earth between

107

him and you.'

Jean Gomper carefully noted these recommendations.

At first he was somewhat disorientated. Everywhere, he could see enormous iron wheels turning, turning. He was in a daze. There was a suffocating smell of burning flesh. He tried, nevertheless, to orientate himself as well as he could, and, after an hour's walk, he reached a long alley lined on either side with red-hot arm-chairs. The damned were sitting in these arm-chairs, their bodies motionless, but their faces writhing in ceaseless agony. It was amongst them that Jean Gomper eventually found his landlord:

'How are you,' he said to him, raising his hat politely.

'Ah! It's you! A curse on you,' cried the damned one. 'It's because of you that I'm here. You've come for your receipt, haven't you? Fool! If you hadn't let go of your money so stupidly, neither I nor my son would have been tempted.'

Whilst saying all this, he had pulled a piece of paper from his pocket:

'Here's your receipt.'

'Excuse me, sir, but that's not the one.'

'Then it must be this one,' said the landlord, showing him a second one.

'It's not that one, either.'

'Ah, you bore me to tears.'

'Let's try the third.'

'Here it is. Take it, you nincompoop.'

'With pleasure, but first put it on the ground.'

The landlord did so.

'Thanks and good luck,' said Jean Gomper as he picked up the paper and folded it carefully.

'I want nothing of your thanks nor your wishes, but would you perhaps do me a favour?'

'Of course, as long as it's not to change places with you.'

'You see this empty chair next to mine? Warn my son it's reserved for him if he carries on following my example.'

And Jean Gomper retraced his footsteps. A boiling sweat ran down his limbs. Suddenly, he felt a breath of fresh air on his face, and there he was in the vicar's dining room.

'Go home,' said the vicar, 'and don't complain again about God not being just.'

Next day, Jean Gomper went to his landlord's son and told him his father's words, then he took the receipt to the man, who accepted it as valid."

(Told by Hervé Brelivet, Quimper, 1888).